Contents

Prologue: The Author and His Work

By John Shook and Durward Sobek

It is with great enthusiasm that we introduce to you a set of important ideas and the man behind them. It is with equally great sadness that we do so posthumously.

Allen Ward completed this manuscript in August 2001. He died in a plane crash in May 2004. In the interim, he continued to work on his ideas—trying them out, arguing them, revising them. Though his theories continued to evolve and grow with great dynamism with each new experience, we think this volume is a good representation of Allen Ward's thinking.

We, John Shook and Durward Sobek, first met Al, as friends and acquaintances knew him, in the early 1990s, when he was an assistant professor of mechanical engineering at the University of Michigan (UM). John was general manager of planning and administration at the Toyota Technical Center, USA, the North American engineering and product development arm of the Toyota Motor Corporation, where a team of UM researchers had converged to embark on a major series of research projects. John had been contacted by Professor John Campbell, who had obtained funding from the U.S. Air Force Office of Scientific Research (AFOSR) to create the university's Japan Technology Management Program. The research team included, among others, Professor of Industrial and Operations Engineering Jeff Liker, whose continuing research led to his landmark publication of *The Toyota Way*; and later, a young graduate student, Durward.

Members of the UM group seemed to fall into one of two camps. Many were researching Toyota to mine what they could find in that company for new concepts or practices. They hoped to analyze and perhaps model them in some way with the aim of presenting an objective picture of what Toyota is and does. The other camp was not that interested in Toyota but knew a good source of research funding when they saw it (the AFOSR in this case) and thought they might be able to get a paper or two published out of it.

Al was completely and obviously different from either group. He had already determined—from ideas developed during his Ph.D. research in artificial intelligence at Massachusetts Institute of Technology (MIT)—that the way product development had

been conducted in conventional systems was fundamentally flawed. Further, based on this theory, he thought he knew *how* it was flawed *and* how to fix it. But he also had a nagging concern: He had never found a real-world example of an organization that consistently operated according to his thinking. Al was looking for a company, just one, that did things the *right* way. When Al first set foot in Toyota, he knew immediately that he had found what he had been seeking, and more.

Later, with Al and Jeff Liker as advisors, Durward completed a Ph.D. dissertation that painted a comprehensive picture of Toyota's product development organization and practices compared and contrasted with those of (then) Chrysler Corporation. Though the comparisons were broad ranging and included detailed descriptions of the organization, leadership approach, communication styles, processes, and philosophy toward design, Al never was fully satisfied. In fact, when Durward met Al for a mock dissertation defense near the end of his program, Al's verdict was, "This is not Ph.D. material." You can imagine Durward's disappointment—even more than that, he was incredulous!

Durward passed the defense later that week, graduated, and became an engineering professor at Montana State University. But, in retrospect, Al was right. The dissertation lacked something.

In some ways, the volume you hold in your hands is the dissertation that Al wanted to see. It draws upon much of the data from Durward's Toyota work, but more importantly, it has that something that was missing. It has deep *insight*.

This book makes a bold statement about the state of engineering leadership in most organizations; about how we view engineering and product/process development; about learning, knowledge, and respect; about human nature, innovation, and personal growth; indeed, about what we value most as players in the product development game. As we will try to convince you in the next few pages, and as you will discover on your own as you read its pages, this book is like no other in the product development literature. What makes it stand apart, and what we think you'll find most valuable, is the depth of insight Allen Ward had into the key foundations of highly effective, lean product development systems.

About the Author

Allen Ward's academic résumé begins with a bachelor's degree in history from the University of Oregon. He always maintained an interest in history and often used historical references in his arguments and explanations of whatever issues he studied. Upon college graduation, he joined the U.S. Army where he served 10 years. He proudly completed combat leadership training at the U.S. Army Ranger School in Fort Benning, Ga., and later toured Korea and attained the rank of Captain. While stationed in Hawaii, he completed a second bachelor's degree in mechanical engineering. From there, Al left the Army and entered MIT as a Ph.D. student. He joined a group in the artificial intelligence laboratory interested in developing tools to automate mechanical engineering design tasks. He developed a prototype software tool and in the process stumbled upon a new design theory he called set-based design.

During his time at UM, Al pursued an aggressive research agenda. Some of his students were developing design automation software that put his theory into computer code, leading Al to discover that standard set propagation theory was inadequate for multidimensional design problems. So other students were developing new mathematical representations and logical operations to tackle these problems. Still other students were working on enhancing existing design methodologies using his new theory. And finally, Al was interested to know if any human engineers practiced a form of his set-based design theory, the interest that led him to Toyota and affiliates.

Al's first trip to Toyota's headquarters in Japan was in 1993, with Yasuko Ward—his wife and a Ford Motor Company engineer—serving as interpreter. The ideas and hypotheses flew fast and furiously. The hypotheses were helpful to John, who was himself trying to figure how to conceptualize and articulate Toyota's product development system. Unlike the company's manufacturing processes—already famous by that time as the Toyota Production System—the product development system had never been fully described. Even inside the company, while engineers and managers understood concretely how the system worked and how to manage it effectively, describing it simply and holistically was another matter.

This topic became the subject of Durward's Ph.D. research. Durward studied Japanese intensively for a year-and-a-half, then spent six months in Japan interviewing Toyota engineers and engineering managers about all aspects of Toyota's product development system. Towards the end of this stay, Al made another study trip to Japan, sleeping on *tatami* mats in Durward's apartment to save money. This cost-saving measure had an unexpected side benefit: Discussion of the day's interviews continued into the long hours of the evening. The research continued after the trip as we interviewed American and Japanese engineers working in Toyota's U.S. operations in Ann Arbor, Mich., and Erlanger, Ky. The preliminary synthesis of the ideas for this book began during the many hours of debate, clarification, and theory-building Al and Durward had while preparing presentations and workshops based on the Toyota research.

As Durward was finishing his Ph.D. work, Al left academia and started a consulting and specialty machine design company. In this capacity, he was in the unique position to: a) observe conventional product development systems in many companies, b) continue to contemplate and develop the ideas that came out of the Toyota research, c) experiment with the ideas in his own design activities, and d) learn by helping companies try out the concepts and dramatically improve performance. Over the ensuing years, John had the opportunity to work with Al to assist companies in their pursuit to become lean enterprises. John was often Al's sounding board. As he discovered each new aspect of Toyota's product development world—or just of Toyota—Al would offer up his analysis or assessment. Before the hypotheses, though, were always the questions, such as: "Lean is about eliminating waste, so what is 'waste' in product development and why is it that engineers never talk about it?" "Does the lean concept of 'takt time' apply to the product development world?" "How much of an engineer's time is spent doing actual engineering work? How much of his or her time *should* be spent doing engineering work?" Through discussing and even arguing these ideas, slowly but steadily a comprehensive sense of "Lean Product Development" began to emerge.

Work continued, and the pace quickened, as more companies became intrigued with his ideas and sought his consulting help. The ideas continued to evolve, and were reflected in his presentation materials to clients and in his workshops. Business continued to pick up. He hired a team of bright young graduates to support him, was in the process of capturing his knowledge in the form of interactive video, and was brimming over with enthusiasm for his work. To become more efficient and serve his clients better, and at the same time pursue a lifelong love of flying, Allen purchased a light aircraft with which he could fly between client locations without being beholden to the schedules and routes of the commercial airlines. Tragically, en route to deliver a workshop at a west coast client's site, Allen Ward and the two passengers on board died in an airplane crash on May 31, 2004.

Why We're Publishing This Book Now

Al created this manuscript in 2001. Searching through his papers and files, we think this manuscript represents the most complete and concise record of his ideas and insights. Rereading it now, we're struck anew with the power and relevance of the ideas as presented in these pages.

- He asks basic questions that drive at the fundamentals of product development.

- He observes the sources (a.k.a., "wastes") of the most common maladies that plague many product development organizations.

- He distills what might be termed "cornerstones" from the practices of lean product developers, most notably Toyota and its partners, which differ remarkably from conventional practice.

- He uniquely melds observations of effective teamwork from his military background, engineering fundamentals from his education and personal experience, design methodology from his research, and theories about management, cognition, and learning from his understanding of history and interactions with clients.

- He carries the implications of his theories into specific, practical recommendations.

- He employs systems thinking in all aspects of thought and investigation.

Much research has been conducted on, and a great deal written about, product development over the last 15 to 20 years. This work runs the gamut, from sophisticated analytical models focused on some narrow aspect of development, to sweeping attempts to describe product development as a complete system; and from tools to aid specific development tasks such as developing customer requirements or devising project plans, to involved statistical analysis relating certain practices or organizational characteristics to measures of performance such as number of patents filed, market share, or sales growth. Nearly all of this work has been conducted within the same set of paradigms, paradigms so deeply engrained that they most often are taken for granted or, in some cases, not even recognized. Al believed a number of them are fundamentally flawed, if not in concept then in implementation. If that's the case, then a set of new paradigms could radically alter forever the way we think about product development. This book represents Allen Ward's proposal for a new set of paradigms.

Of course, there is still plenty of room for debate and additional investigation; but if the ideas are not publicized, we might forever lose the opportunity to have that debate and thereby not benefit from the life's work of a gifted scholar and engineer—a second tragedy that makes the first even worse.

But there is a problem. The manuscript Al left was not quite finished. We also know that his thinking evolved beyond that captured in the manuscript, and that some of the examples used are a few years out of date. Yet the ideas are powerful, the insights valuable, and the recommendations potentially revolutionary—how can we get this out where people can read it, debate it, and put it to profitable use?

Our approach was to leave the manuscript as intact as possible, in order to preserve the author's original intent and, to the extent possible, reflect his personality. We have done minimal editing solely to improve readability and flow. We also added a few editorial notes where we think additional clarification may be useful to the reader. Finally, we wrote this introduction to place the work in an appropriate context to help the reader better appreciate the material and its presentation; specifically, to fill in a couple of gaps that probably would've been filled in subsequent versions.

What you will find as you read these pages is a prose that reflects Al's personality and style. He will tell you in no uncertain terms what he believes, and tell you what he believes *you* should do. He will look you in the eye to see if you blink. At times, he is pedantic, which may offend some readers (we hope not; though, on the other hand, Al probably would not have minded—he liked to issue challenges, and sometimes they would sting!). Like a tough professor, he suggests assignments that are probably unrealistically difficult. As a purely academic work, this book as it is might not stand as rigorous research. But ivory tower academic "rigor" was not what Al was about. He was about understanding, insight, and the rigor of engineering as a discipline in the real world. Following is an overview of some of the insight Al will share.

The Foundations of Lean Product and Process Development

If we are going to design high-performing, super-efficient product-process development systems, we need razor-sharp clarity on some fundamental questions:

- What is the purpose of product development?
- What does it produce?
- What is a good development system?
- What is "value" (or "value added" or "value creating") in product development?

It is Al's opinion (and we agree), most companies have poor answers to these questions! And if we do not have good clarity on, for example, what exactly does a product development process produce, how can we possibly do it well? Thus the first insights are in the answers to these fundamental questions.

This discussion of basic questions then leads directly to a set of proposed performance measures for product development. The author's second insight is that many product development organizations evaluate and reward the wrong things. Thus most of Part 1 describes six measures for evaluating product development effectiveness.

In Part 2, the author shares his observation that many product development organizations are hopelessly out of control (in "death spirals" of one sort or another). A death spiral in product development might look like this: Engineers in a company are overburdened and facing management pressure to meet deadlines. They overlook things or cut corners to meet management's expectations, and mistakes occur. In response, management implements more checks in the system to try to catch the mistakes, usually consisting of more reviews and reports. This creates more work for the engineers, increasing their burden, resulting in more mistakes (or missed deadlines). So more checks are put in place, and the cycle continues until the organization is crippled and management decides product development is no longer a "core competence."

Further, conventional thinking often makes these situations worse because the natural reactions reinforce the downward spiral, as in the example above. At the root of most product development death spirals, Al observes, is a handful of wastes—scatter, hand off, and wishful thinking being the main culprits. The way out of the downward spirals is to attack the wastes at the center of the negatively reinforcing feedback loops. His explanation in Part 2 powerfully demonstrates the inadequacy of conventional thinking, and sets the stage for an entirely new way of thinking about product development.

In Part 3, Al articulates his vision for a totally new approach to product development. The starting point is focusing on value, while noting that the value of product development is in creating useable knowledge and profitable operational value streams. His core thesis is that the very *aim of the product development process is to create profitable operational value streams*, and further, that creating useable knowledge is the key to doing so predictably, efficiently, and effectively. To create useable knowledge requires learning. So the author presents a basic learning model for development that serves as the basis for all product development activity and support structures.

In the book, Al describes a three-part learning cycle for the product developer: Go See —Ask Why—(In)Form. Later in his thinking, though not reflected in this manuscript, Al began to realize the vital importance of this basic learning cycle, and elevated it to one of the five basic principles. He also added a couple more steps that are critical for lean developers, and renamed it the LAMDA principle.

LAMDA stands for:

- Look—as in go and see for yourself,

- Ask—get to the root cause,

- Model—using engineering analysis, simulation, or prototypes,

- Discuss—with peer reviewers, mentors, and developers of interfacing subsystems, and

- Act—test your understanding experimentally.

When you finish the cycle, *Look* again. What Al observed at Toyota and other lean developers is a view of learning and knowledge creation that differs substantially from conventional practice. This view encourages *in situ* observation because problems almost always arise because of a gap between what we think we understand and actuality. It advocates deep investigation, using appropriate engineering tools and principles. It recognizes that knowledge creation and sense-making is often socially co-constructed, and that we have much to learn from each other. And it strongly implies that knowledge must be validated, continually, forever. We encourage the reader to give due consideration to what Al calls, "the fundamental value-creating cycle," as it does not occupy as much space as it might if Al were writing this book today.

He then turns attention to the major pieces of the value stream that must be aligned among themselves and with the customer: development organizational structure, manufacturing system, and suppliers.

The remainder of Part 3, and approximately half of the book, delves into four "cornerstones" of lean product development, each of which turns conventional thinking about product development on its head.

1. *Entrepreneurial System Designer (ESD).* The lean development organization makes one person responsible for the engineering and aesthetic design, and market and business success, of the product. This person cuts across departmental boundaries

to create integration knowledge and bring the organization's focus onto the entire value stream (suppliers through manufacturing to customers). The ESD has little administrative responsibility, and is supported by strong functional groups that have developed deep repositories of knowledge in specialty areas. The ESD leads the development effort to integrate that knowledge into a successful product. This idea runs directly counter to the common paradigm that product development projects should be led by well-oiled, cooperative multidisciplinary teams—not that lean developers don't appreciate teamwork, but how it is implemented in practice is very different.

2. *Teams of Responsible Experts.* Lean product development organizations develop personnel management systems that reward individuals and teams for creating and teaching knowledge that contributes to robust profitability. Functional department heads of the organization lead the knowledge-creating process, and ensure that knowledge capture and dissemination systems work effectively. Interestingly, having strong discipline-focused groups forces a natural tension with the ESD. This seems to differ from many of the undertones of product development literature where words such as "cooperation" and "teamwork" are viewed as positive, and "conflict" viewed as negative. However, Al recognized that this "creative tension" is one of the keys to simultaneously reconciling diverse perspectives and fostering innovation.

3. *Set-Based Concurrent Engineering.* Lean developers recognize that learning rates increase geometrically by considering redundant concepts or design alternatives at every level of the system. This also increases the likelihood of success to the point that, if correctly managed, creates a highly robust, reliable, and therefore predictable product development cycle. However, to avoid eating up excessive amounts of resource, lean developers devise methods to aggressively eliminate weak alternatives. Furthermore, they systematically synthesize learning into design space maps such as trade-off curves—knowledge that can be reused on subsequent projects, with the effect of greatly increasing both the speed and quality of design.

This idea, too, runs counter to a common paradigm: that design is iterative in nature. Thus, product development teams try an idea, analyze it to find its weak points, change it, analyze it again, and so on until they have an acceptable design. The problem is, this almost never works well! Al first introduced the set-based idea in a product development context in a paper about "The Second Toyota Paradox."[a] In it, he and his colleagues argue that a better paradigm for product development is one in which participants reason and communicate about sets of ideas, and gradually narrow those sets to converge on a final design that meets the needs and requirements of everyone concerned. This is the model we observed at Toyota. Still today, 10 years after its publication, Durward gets requests for copies of the article and has faculty members at institutions around the country mention that they still have that article as required reading for their product development or engineering design courses.

4. *Cadence, Pull, and Flow.* Managers of lean development organizations reject the scientific management notion that managers plan, and workers do. Rather, developers plan their own work and work their own plans, under the guidance of a coach. But what do they plan to do? One of management's responsibilities is to release projects on a regular cadence into the organization, in order to level the workload. Projects are defined by integrating events or milestones (set by the ESD), and developers plan their work to meet those events. In this way, engineering work is pulled rather than scheduled. Communication networks are similarly established so that information is pulled by the person needing to know, rather than pushed onto developers according to some centrally planned schedule. The result is the elimination of wasteful management structures and reports, and continuous cycles of improvement and waste reduction.

This last cornerstone takes aim at typical implementations of stage-gate theory for managing development projects. Why? Because they are basically push systems. Toyota already has demonstrated that pull systems are more efficient and profitable than push systems in manufacturing. Al argues that Toyota also has demonstrated it in the development world.

Part 4 brings the book to a close by offering a few suggestions about getting started on the change from conventional to lean. It is brief. Had Al been able to see this book through to publication, we are quite sure that he would've had much more to say here. As it stands, the chapter invites both individual readers and the larger product development community to discuss, experiment, observe, ask why, and experiment some more, to come to their own consensus on how to make the transformation.

---

a. Allen Ward, Jeffrey K. Liker, John J. Cristiano, and Durward K. Sobek II, "The Second Toyota Paradox: How Delaying Decisions Can Make Better Cars Faster," *Sloan Management Review*, Spring 1995, vol. 36, no. 3, pp. 43-61.

Invitation to Read On

With this as background, we invite you to read on, but with some words of advice. First, be warned that the idea density in some sections of this book is very high! Be prepared to take frequent breaks to reflect and fully absorb the ideas, and do not hesitate to reread sections, multiple times if necessary. We did.

Second, we don't necessarily agree with everything Al wrote and don't expect you to either. Nor would Al even want you to. Rather, the purpose of this publication is to introduce some insightful observations and innovative ideas that could potentially change engineering and product design practice fundamentally; while encouraging conversation, discussion, and debate. You may not find all of the arguments compelling, but we hope that you will do more than take them at face value. We hope that you will think deeply about them because, even if in the end you are not convinced, we trust that the exercise of having done so will prove beneficial.

Third, we encourage you to not stop at discussion, but to actually get your hands dirty and try these ideas. Some of the exercises suggested may sound overwhelming, but we still encourage you to give them a try, even if a scaled-down version (for example, the assignment may suggest doing something for all of your company's products, which may be daunting; but maybe you could do it for one product family). If they don't work as expected, investigate the root cause, and experiment some more. After all, if the current system is in a death spiral, doing the same things more earnestly will only make things worse.

It is our honor and privilege to present this work as a final farewell to our colleague, mentor, and friend. We hope you are blessed by him in this volume as we were in knowing him. We can think of no more fitting tribute.

Al's ideas have continued to have life and influence since his untimely passing. We hope this volume will introduce Al's important ideas to as broad an audience as possible. Al would never ask that you take everything between the covers of this book as gospel. All he would ask is that you take the ideas seriously, give them a try, challenge them where you disagree, and take it upon yourself to push the thinking forward in new, perhaps unexpected, directions. He would want you to listen, change the way you think and work, and then argue passionately about what you've tried that worked, what didn't, and why. We are convinced that anyone who gives the ideas serious thought and even a try will find them as rewarding as Al's students and colleagues already know them to be. Now prepare yourself for a fascinating journey, with Allen Ward as your captain!

John Shook   Durward K. Sobek II
Ann Arbor, Mich.   Bozeman, Mont.
January 2, 2007

Introduction

What I'm trying to do

I wrote this book to answer a question: How can you make all of your development projects make a lot more money—and have more fun at the same time?

You may be a CEO, a working engineer, a middle manager, or a lean change agent. Lean development is a revolutionary-but-proven system that could:

- Reduce your development time and resources use as much as four times.

- Reduce the risk of quality problems, schedule and cost overruns, and failed products as much as 10 times.

- Increase innovation as much as 10 times.

- Re-use production systems and parts, slashing capital costs and improving quality.

The total effect should be to make all of your projects provide return on investment equal to or better than your best current projects. Hard to believe? We'll scrutinize the data in Part 1.

The Toyota Motor Corporation and its suppliers created the lean development system. That took most of a century, and they still are learning. Lean development helped to make Toyota so successful that Toyota's total market stock value (shares X price) exceeds all of the rest of the world's auto companies' stock combined. Yet, unlike Toyota's famous lean manufacturing system, lean development is little known outside of the Toyota circle.

Fortunately, there is nothing inherently Japanese, mysterious, or specific to automobiles about lean development. You will have to tune the application of these ideas to your situation; but the ideas themselves are based on human nature and universal logic.

Development is different from manufacturing. John Shook, the first American to work for Toyota in Japan, believes that lean development in some ways reveals Toyota's secrets better than lean manufacturing. Lean development shares many fundamental concepts with the lean thinking expounded by Jim Womack and Dan Jones, and it is extremely efficient. But other names would work: fast development, robust development, responsibility-based development, or knowledge-based development.

Whatever we call it, lean development is based on one simple-but-revolutionary idea, and here it is.

The basic secret

Lean development's goal is learning fast how to make good products. "*That's it?*" you say. "*Some secret.*" Ah, but only Toyota has spent a century building a development process around the goal of learning. Conventional development is built around getting people to follow orders.

Consider Henry Ford and Kiichiro Toyoda. Both were technical geniuses and visionaries. Both passionately wanted to create car companies. But their situations were totally different.

Detroit was a major industrial center, and Ford could hire skilled machinists, mechanics, millwrights, and foremen to engineer products and meticulously design the production systems that produced them. The United States had great universities educating engineers, and he could hire the best. Also, Ford was an extraordinarily experienced craftsman; he had built cars and engines, founded previous companies, and moved from job to job for 20 years to gain experience. So he could give orders. The orders were more or less right, they were more or less followed, and they more or less worked.

- Ford used scientific management, which says there is one best way to do anything, and an expert can find it. Then, managers can tell the people who actually do the work to follow the process. (In Part 2 we'll learn to call this the *waste of hand-off*.) Ford told people, "Do as I tell you." Scientific management was a great fit to mass production.[1]

1. The author uses a definition of the term "scientific management" based on his perception of the modern-day implementation of the concept. This definition is not necessarily the same as that of Frederick Taylor, who originally coined the term in the early 1900s.

(Am I over-simplifying? Maybe—but I hope I'm just revealing the underlying simplicity that always was there.)

Kiirchiro Toyoda, in his effort to create a car company, had a much harder problem. He had little experience—six months of touring the United States. He was located in a small village with little industry. Tokyo University produced relatively few engineers, and they mostly stayed in Tokyo and worked for Nissan.

No one around Toyota knew how to build a car; how to cast an engine; how to design an engine; how to make steel suitable for bodies; how to stamp it; how to make a stamping die. Toyota made its first car bodies by digging a hole in the ground in the shape of an upside-down car and beating the metal into it with hammers.[2]

So Toyoda couldn't give successful orders. He didn't know what to tell people to do. If he had, they wouldn't have known how to do it. He had to tell people, "We are going to build cars. Let's all learn as much as we can, as fast as we can, and work together to create something our customers will buy. My job is the same as yours: to learn as fast as I can."

Scientific/conventional management actually is based on two 17th century assumptions: Order in any system must be created by a greater intelligence operating from outside the system, and systems are predictable. So, management's job is to tell people to follow the one best way. The company then will run as designed.

Unfortunately for conventional management, the 17th century was wrong. Actually, modern science shows that order emerges from interactions inside certain kinds of systems, and most systems are *not* predictable. Therefore, lean management's job is to continuously help order emerge by learning and helping others to learn. And Toyota is the first 21st century company to do that.

Once you learn how, lean management is a lot easier than telling people what to do. You don't have to pretend to know everything, and it works. You can spend your time creating value—what customers actually want—instead of drowning in the waste created by conventional-management theory.

As we'll see in Part 4, you can adopt the system a little at a time, but you do need to focus on the system.

---

2. The editors have not been able to verify this statement.

The system, and how I learned it

I've been a soldier, an artificial intelligence researcher, a university professor, an engineering cog in a corporate machine, and owner and chief engineer of a machine design and build company. A common thread ran through those experiences: We were doing something wrong. Somehow, despite all of our efforts, nothing ever went quite right. We commanded, we expedited, we planned—and all of our thrashing seemed to create as much frustration as progress. It took me a long time to recognize the solution when I saw it.

I stumbled across Toyota's development system while trying to prove a theory. I was an assistant professor in mechanical engineering at the University of Michigan.

Earlier, doing design automation research at Massachusetts Institute of Technology's Artificial Intelligence Lab, I'd developed a concept called *set-based concurrent engineering* (SBCE). To use my "mechanical design compiler" program, you gave it a schematic and specifications. The program had modules representing the cataloged components to go in the schematic motors, transmissions, hydraulic pumps, etc. Instead of picking components and changing them if they didn't work, the modules sent each other summaries off all of the alternatives. They eliminated bad alternatives by proving they couldn't work or were inferior to a proven solution.

This worked so well that I thought maybe other people should use SBCE too. When I came to Michigan, I found an interested sociologist named Jeff Liker. In 1991, we surveyed auto builders and suppliers in the United States and Japan, looking for SBCE. We found it—at Toyota.

Fortunately, Toyota welcomed the opportunity to explain its success, probably because of worry about U.S. protectionism. We and our graduate students (especially Durward Sobek, now a professor at Montana State University) went back repeatedly. In addition to SBCE, we saw a lot at Toyota that I *wasn't* looking for:

- A clear understanding of *value* in product development—usable knowledge— and a relentless focus on creating it.

- Project leaders acting as entrepreneurs and system designers—not as bureaucratic managers.

- A simple project management system built on the principles of cadence, pull, and flow.

- A *team of responsible experts* taking the initiative, learning, teaching, negotiating, and creating.

And all of these characteristics fit together into a smoothly operating system.

To my surprise, I realized I had seen this before when similar principles guided the U.S. Army to recovery after Vietnam and swift victory in the Persian Gulf during Operation Desert Storm. Lean development isn't Japanese. Most of it isn't even limited to development.

But the Army's description of the principles is tuned for war, not development, and Toyota never wrote the principles down. Toyota teaches lean development by apprenticeship. The more than 100 Toyota and supplier engineers and managers we interviewed were generous with insights about why the system works—and their insights were all different.

I've tried to synthesize those insights into a coherent system. When I present these concepts at Toyota, American and Japanese employees react differently. The Japanese usually say something like, "On slide 48 you said that we do X; now we do Y instead." The Americans say, "Now I understand!"

Lean development goes beyond lean manufacturing principles and beyond conventional "concurrent engineering" methods. Indeed, Toyota makes little use of such concurrent engineering methods as design of experiments, co-located and dedicated teams, quality function deployment charts, or design for manufacture software. But collectively, Toyota's methods produce remarkable results. As we will see in Part 1, Toyota is about twice as fast, twice as efficient, and twice as profitable as its best U.S. competitors.

Better, cheaper, faster—why would anyone do anything else? Because there has been no way to understand the system as a whole.

Why you need this book

U.S. companies have tried to use lean development. Every U.S. auto company has studied Toyota's development methods. Liker, our students, and I wrote papers for the *Harvard Business Review* and *Sloan Management Review*. They won the Shingo Prize and have been read widely. Chrysler Corporation has attempted to apply set-based methods. All three U.S. automakers have adopted versions of Toyota's project-leadership approach. General Motors Corporation has tried to "standardize" engineering work, believing this imitates Toyota. Yet design quality problems, long project lead times, and high development costs persist—and U.S. auto profits and market share rapidly are declining again.

I've had some dramatic successes working with clients over the last four years—but the conventional system seems to creep back in whenever I turn my back. We get pieces of the lean system in place; they work (usually); and then all of a sudden they are gone again.

I think these failures come because people haven't had any way to understand the whole system—and they've often misunderstood the pieces. Ford Motor Company and GM appointed heavy-weight project managers —"like Toyota's"—without understanding why Toyota's project leaders primarily are system designers. So, the project managers became one more cog in the bureaucracy.

Jim Luckman led the most advanced lean development implementation outside of the Toyota circle at the Delphi Automotive Systems Rochester Technical Center. He puts it this way: "Unless you keep spreading the virus, the immune system of the organization will reject it."

This book is designed to provide a clear overview of the entire system, so that you won't get it partly implemented, get stuck on a missing piece, and fall back into conventional patterns. You can start change where it feels best; just don't stop. Don't ever stop. Part of lean development is that you keep learning how to do it better, forever.

You'll *unlearn* as much as you learn. For example, an American manager at the Toyota Georgetown, Ky., plant said, "It took me three years to stop yelling at people." Yelling at people was what he had always done. Yelling worked. He was good at yelling. Toyota-style management required him to stop doing things that worked and that he was good at, and learn to do completely different things.

Right now, you and your company are unconsciously incompetent at lean development; you don't know what you don't know. By the end of the book, you'll be consciously incompetent. You'll know what you have to learn to do, and you'll have a plan for learning, one concept at a time. For a while, you'll apply each concept consciously, slowly, carefully. You'll be consciously competent. And then it will become second nature. You'll be unconsciously competent, and you'll go on to further concepts.

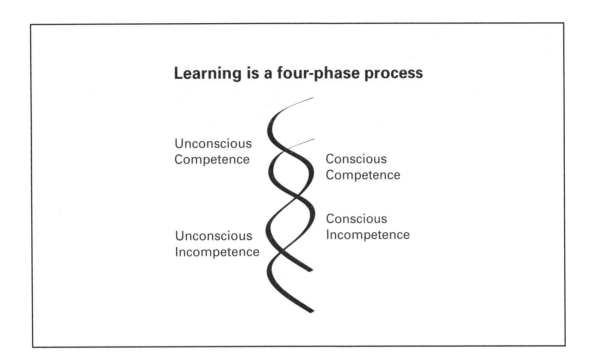

Learning is a four-phase process

Unconscious Competence

Conscious Competence

Unconscious Incompetence

Conscious Incompetence

How this book is organized

Part 1 lays the foundation by asking, "What is value in development?" Once we know what value is, we can design the rest of the system to produce it. Part 1 also provides some ways for you to measure how well you are doing and estimate how much you can improve. This can help build the case for change (you will need to persuade a lot of people before you are done).

Part 2 shows you how to find "knowledge waste." If you understand the waste in conventional development, lean development will make more sense, and you'll be eager to apply it.

Part 3 provides a detailed overview of the entire lean development system, so that you can formulate your own vision of the future. What do you want your development system to be? This is the longest part of the book.

Part 4 provides methods for making the change so that lean development doesn't become just another "program of the month."

Boxes that are shaded

suggest things you should do. These instructions deliberately are brief and simple, so just plunge ahead, and you'll find you can do the job. Don't try to do everything at once—but I recommend that you create your own list as you read and do them as soon as you can.

The lean development system works. It makes money. It's fun because it lets you concentrate on creating value instead of managing waste. It is much simpler and more straightforward than conventional methods—once you understand it. It is based on sound principles that work everywhere, from creating art to the crucibles of combat.

Let's get to work.

Part 1: Value and Performance

What *value* does development create? How can you tell how good your system is? How much better could it be?

In *Lean Thinking*, Womack and Jones told us to figure out what value is—what customers actually want—and concentrate on "value streams"—the connected activities that create value. Conventional companies often get so involved in their internal organization that they lose sight of value and produce waste instead. Lean companies focus on value streams to eliminate nonvalue-adding activities. We'll be concerned with the *development* value stream and *operational* value stream.

The *operational value stream* includes activities converting raw material to products in the hands of customers. The operational value stream produces high-quality products at the time the customer wants them. Activities are *value-creating* when they change materials toward the products customers pay for.

The *development value stream* includes activities running from recognizing an opportunity through manufacturing launch.

Here's the preview of this part of the book:

- Development creates operational value streams. Operations divisions are its primary customers. Good development systems consistently create profitable value streams.

- Development creates two kinds of value: manufacturing systems and usable knowledge.

- Development performance can be measured by the consistent profitability of the operational value streams it produces; by the resources it consumes; and by the rate at which it generates usable knowledge.

- Lean companies perform better on all of these measures. Their developments are better, more reliable, cheaper, and faster.

Producing profitable operational value streams

First, what does development produce? When I ask, developers give conflicting and confusing answers. (I'm going use the word "developer" to mean anyone involved in the development process: managers, engineers, stylists and industrial designers, programmers and project managers.) Some say the development system creates drawings and analysis. It does—but do customers pay for these? If not, what good is development? Some say that the development system creates products. But all the products that I buy come from factories. (For a few, one-off products the development and operational value streams are combined, of course.)

No wonder conventional companies don't develop very well. They don't know what they are trying to develop!

Development

Profitable Operational Value Stream

The development value stream produces operational value streams. Operational value streams run from suppliers through factories into product features and out to customers. They don't exist until development processes create them. Drawings, analysis, and tests have value if they create quality operational value streams. So, operations departments are the primary customers of the development value stream. Development has value only if it enables operations to deliver better products to the external customer. Operations departments are the primary customers for development.

In conventional development, Operations is at the bottom of the totem pole. Marketing creates specifications; Product Engineering designs products to meet those specifications; Manufacturing Engineering figures out how to make those products; and the plant tries to execute these manufacturing plans. Each party in this sequence complains that the downstream parties haven't performed as demanded. One sometimes hears, "*It's a good product, but we can't make it with consistently high quality.*" What?!? If it doesn't satisfy the customer, how can it be a good product?

 Make Operations Your Customer

Explain to everyone who needs to hear: "*We don't make money until customers buy what comes out of our plants. Development exists to create operational value streams. Operations is our customer. We should listen to and serve operations just like external customers.*"

A good development value stream consistently produces profitable operational value streams. "*Wait!*" you say. "*No fair! What if our industry is in a slump? What if our plant managers are idiots? You can't hold development responsible for that!*"

O.K. To evaluate development generously, focus on *consistency*. Compare average project return on investment against your best projects' return on investment. After all, you know that the market and the operations department are capable of producing the highest ROI. Any variation is coming out of development. While you're at it, try to compare yourself to the best projects in the industry.

Instruments for evaluating development

We've come to our first instruments for evaluating development. Most of the instruments will be presented in pairs: a retrospective instrument you can use to identify past problems, and a prospective estimate you can use to make decisions.

1. Projected and actual return on investment.

There are a lot of ways to calculate project return on investment (ROI)[3], depending on whether you incorporate taxes, interest rates, etc.

---

3. This equation assumes the following: all "investment" (engineering, development, tooling costs) occurs as a lump sum at the beginning of the project, all "earnings" occur as a lump sum at the end of the project, and interest does not compound. ROI is annualized if project life is expressed in years. These assumptions produce a fairly conservative ROI estimate.

Here's a simple equation you can use:

$$ROI = \frac{\text{earnings-investment}}{\text{total life X investment}}$$

Where:
- earnings = (lifetime sales) X (price – cost)
- cost is the cost of manufacturing, shipping, warranty, sales commissions, etc., per product
- total life runs from the beginning of the project to the date the product stops selling, and investment includes at least engineering and tooling costs

Obviously, more sophisticated analysis would explicitly include the timing of expenditures and incomes, the cost of money, changes in prices and costs, etc. More importantly, estimating lifetime sales is tricky. See Reinertsen, *Managing the Design Factory*, for some ideas.

However you do it, three points are important:

- Treat development costs as an investment.

- Use projected ROI as an instrument to observe the development system and guide decisions, not a metric to evaluate and reward individuals (actual ROI may be robust enough that you can use it to evaluate developers.).

- Keep the ROI model simple enough for developers to understand and use in daily work.

Let's look at these points in detail.

- Development investment includes tooling investment, but also engineering costs, costs of arranging suppliers, costs of installing the tooling in the plant, and sales costs if the product is sold before being manufactured. (Leave out whatever won't affect decisions to keep the model simple.) Tax law and generally accepted accounting practice treat most of these costs as current expenses, not investments. But they are investments, whatever the IRS says. We wouldn't do them if we didn't hope for a future return, and we can't wisely manage development unless we treat them that way.

- Many companies make decisions based on unit profit sales price minus manufacturing costs, possibly including equipment depreciation. But this leaves out the very cost we must manage in development cost.

- Project teams and development managers should use projected profitability as their primary tool in decisions about product features, timing, and resource allocation. But don't pressure teams to produce high projected ROI or "make a business case." They will "bend the needle on the instrument," and make it useless.

- Use the estimate as an advanced indicator of problems with the development process, and ask project team members to help identify the root cause of expected low profits. Cancel projects if projected ROI on the investment to come still is low. (The money already spent is sunk costs—ignore it when making decisions.)

In a lean organization, we want people to see the effect of their work, so that we don't have to tell them what to do. Simple, universally used profit measures help create an information field that guides people to do the right thing.

So, how good is Toyota's development process at creating profitable operational value streams? Year in and year out, Toyota makes more money per vehicle than any other producer. This is astonishing, because:[4]

- Toyota's home market is so deep in prolonged recession that every Japanese automaker except Toyota and Honda is nearly bankrupt. Toyota, by contrast, has about US$40 billion in the bank, more than all U.S. automakers combined.

- Toyota until recently lagged in large pickups and sport utility vehicles—it earns these high profits on cars. No U.S. automaker earns significant profits on cars—enthusiasm for SUV and light trucks accounts for all the high U.S. profitability of the past few years. (As I write, Toyota has entered the large light truck market with the Tundra, having built U.S. plants to avoid triggering protectionism. Toyota sales in the U.S. are up 16% over last year; U.S. company sales are down 6%.)

- The entire automotive world is trying to copy Toyota's lean manufacturing system, so that Toyota's manufacturing advantage is decreasing.

But we can't consider ROI in isolation. A company can achieve high ROI in a death spiral because it is not investing. So, an even better leading indicator is market share change.

4. These assertions were the author's understanding at the time of writing.

Projected and Actual Change in Market Share

Along with consistently high profit, Toyota's development system steadily increases world market share. Toyota's major suppliers, such as Denso, also have been steadily increasing world market share, while maintaining high profits. But how do they do it?

Profits and market-share growth are high when there are few "defective" projects that run over schedule or budget, have significant quality or cost problems, or miss the market.

 DO

Use project ROI and market share change to manage development

Many companies don't track project ROI, and you may have to make rough estimates of engineering investment. Use ROI as your primary guide for investment decisions within and between projects. (Don't just shoot for a minimum acceptable ROI; constantly monitor your decisions to achieve maximum ROI.)

Toyota and its suppliers have consistently successful projects. They analyze the few defective projects to improve the system. Morale is high and chaos low because projects *consistently* go right.

In contrast, most conventional projects have serious problems and an occasional home run keeps the company afloat. Fire fighting is standard. It is hard to tell who is doing a good job and hard even to tell what the causes of the problems are. Waves of disruption run through the company, as projects are canceled, run over budget or schedule, or must be expedited to make up for failures elsewhere. Everyone is worried all the time. Thus, we have another instrument:

2a. Project defect rates.

If you could eliminate project defects in your company, how much would you gain? To repeat: you know that a well-designed operational value stream—plants, suppliers, and customers—is capable of producing the profitability of the best projects in your industry. Weak project ROI is a consequence of development defects, which the lean system should eliminate. A lean development process should move your average ROI close to the best ROI of conventional projects. If your best projects earn 20% ROI, and your average is 5%, you ought to be able to increase profitability by a factor of four just by eliminating project defects.

 DO **Use project defect rate to spur change**

Determine your project defect rate. Plot the distribution of ROIs for recent projects, color coding for defective and completely successful projects. Compute how much more money you would make if all projects returned the maximum ROI. Publicize this in internal media, or post it in halls; use it to agitate for lean development.

I need to emphasize something here. Improving the system to prevent defects does NOT mean adding more tests, analysis, signatures, gates, or controls to the system. These things make developers work harder, in an effort to prevent a particular problem from reoccurring. But the basic problem is that every developer I know already is working too hard, so things "fall through the cracks." Improving the system means making things easier for developers, not harder.

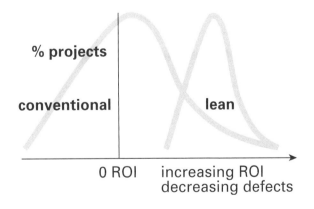

To evaluate my belief that lean development should nearly eliminate defective projects, let's look at the data for specific failure modes.

Market miss: Markets are missed because the development team fails to understand the customer, or because it is not innovative enough. The only hard U.S. data on innovation in lean development comes from one team at the Delphi Rochester Technical Center, which achieved a 10-fold increase in patent applications over conventional process norms. We also know that Toyota is capable of extraordinary innovations that squarely hit real markets:

- The first Lexus aimed at a market segment in which Toyota had never competed; it was widely hailed as the best car in the world.

- The Prius hybrid-electric vehicle is the biggest change in automotive technology in a century.

- Denso also has demonstrated unusual ability to invent to schedule. For example, one Denso team set out to reduce radiator weight by 50%, while enabling radiator cores for every vehicle size to be produced on the same machine. They succeeded.

Cost and quality problems: These problems appear in the factory and the field, but are usually caused by poor development. We know that:

- Toyota consistently has the world's highest quality.

- Denso has never had a product recall.[5]

Of course, quality as measured by surveys of initial product defects is due partly to the manufacturing system—though even this is affected strongly by design for manufacture and integration of manufacturing system development into product development. But long-term quality—the extraordinary durability and maintainability of even low-cost Toyota products—is almost entirely a function of development.

Time and budget overruns: Toyota people have told me that they never miss a launch date, though they occasionally adjust one! Seriously, Toyota normally allows only two weeks to ramp up from the first car produced to full-rate production; U.S. automakers may need six months. Projects finish on time and in budget with striking consistency. U.S. results have not been as good, but still substantially better than in conventional projects.

5. This was the author's understanding at the time of writing.

I have all the teams I work with estimate the probability of a significant product defect. The probability of complete success using conventional methods is almost always under 30%. Experience bears this out as 80% of conventional projects experience a serious defect.

We have another instrument:

2b. Estimated probability of failure.

These estimates are easy:

1. If possible, break the system into subsystems or components.

2. Identify failure modes for each subsystem, and the system as a whole.

3. Guesstimate the probability that each failure mode won't cause a defective project.

4. Multiply these probabilities to find the probability of a successful, non-defective project.

For example:

Subsystem & failure mode	Probability of success
Whole system	
Parts don't fit.	0.9
Assembly defects.	0.9
Subsystem A	
Customers don't like it.	0.8
Supplier delays project.	0.9
Subsystem B	
Not strong enough.	0.8
Total Probability of Success =	0.47

This procedure tends to over-estimate the probability of success, because there are always failure modes you didn't think of.

Start using probability of failure

Get your project teams to use estimated probability of failure to guide their actions. They can (and should) reduce their probability of failure below 5% by using set-based concurrent engineering, which is discussed in Part 3.

So you've learned enough to assess how good your system is. Now, it is time to take your analysis of the cause of poor profits one step deeper.

Focusing on creating knowledge-value

Low ROI and declining market share are caused by defective projects that miss the market, have manufacturing cost or quality problems, or budget and time overruns. But what causes defective projects?

Almost all defective projects result from not having the right knowledge in the right place at the right time. Therefore, usable knowledge is the basic value created during development. Useable knowledge prevents defects, excites customers, and creates profitable operational value streams.

Usable development knowledge is created by three basic kinds of learning:

- *Integration learning* includes learning about customers, suppliers, partners, the physical environment in which the product will be used, etc. It helps us understand how to integrate our designs with the needs of others—most importantly, our customers.

- *Innovation learning* creates new possible solutions.

- *Feasibility learning* enables better decisions among the possible new solutions, avoiding cost and quality problems, or project overruns.

As we'll see in Part 3, making integration and feasibility learning "useable" is a critical part of the process. Lean companies devote a lot of effort to abstracting data into useable knowledge in the form of trade-off curves.

Profit: excited customers, low cost, high quality, on time

innovates   Integrates (internally, and with customers, suppliers, the world)   enables good decisions

Hardware, software

Useful knowledge

Value-adding developer effort

As useable knowledge increases, the amount of new tooling required decreases. Lean companies therefore generally spend a larger fraction of their development effort creating knowledge and a smaller fraction creating hardware. A focus on useable knowledge is the heart of lean development. Part 2 of this book identifies wastes of knowledge. Part 3 shows how the lean system creates knowledge and prevents its waste. Part 4 discusses change as a learning process.

Now that we know what value is, we can ask the obvious question: *How much of our time is spent creating value?*

3. What fraction of developer time is spent creating value?
Most U.S. engineers spend between 10% and 30% of their time creating value; most managers less than 5%. Developers enjoy the value-creating parts of their jobs, and often quit from boredom because their time is being wasted in nonvalue-creating activities. The development system wastes their time.

How much improvement is possible? Consider my discussion with the head of Toyota's Advanced Vehicle Development department, a "general manager" supervising about 150 engineers. I asked how much of his time he spent on administration—personnel paperwork, budget, etc.—and how much on technical work.

He said: *"Don't tell anyone, but I'm getting close to retirement, and I only work 40 hours a week any more. Administration takes two of those. The rest I spend on technical problems. But every technical problem is also a personnel problem, because the problems don't get to me if my people know how to solve them. So all the time I'm solving technical problems, I'm also teaching someone."*

- Three points: First, this senior manager spent most of his time creating value for the product and the company. Second, his solution to personnel problems was to teach. Third, he did not retire, but went on to become a vice president; his behavior was rewarded.[6]

Many managers are afraid that they don't know how to create value. Don't worry—you will by the time you're done with this book.

- Not all nonvalue-creating time is wasted. Toyota distinguishes among value-creating activities (creating usable knowledge or material); nonvalue-adding but necessary activities (NVABN) (e.g., organizing files); and waste.[7]

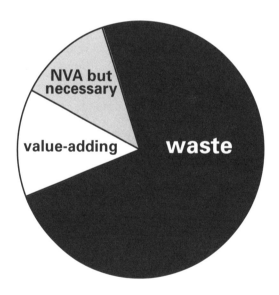

6–7. This was the author's understanding at the time of writing.

Suppose we have 20% value-creating time, and 20% nonvalue-creating but necessary time, with 60% waste time. If we could convert all the waste to value-creating time, we would increase our development throughput by a factor of four, even without making the value-creating processes more efficient. If the rest of the company could keep up, we would be able to increase our profits by the same ratio.

Some of our increased value-creating time will be spent improving quality rather than throughput. However, we'll see most project defects are caused by throwing away knowledge we already have, so most of our increased efficiency can go to increase throughput. Experience supports this. In the year 2000:

- Toyota launched 14 new products—more than GM. In that year Toyota was a company of 70,000 people; GM was a company of 386,000 people.

- Toyota typically used about 300 engineers on a project. The project lasted about two years. Each engineer worked on at least two projects at a time. Conversely, for a major platform project, Chrysler typically dedicated 600 engineers, full time, for around four years.

- The Delphi Rochester Technical Center claimed a throughput increase of 200% over a period of three years by partly implementing lean development, with plenty of additional gains still in sight.

As engineering throughput increases, you'll also need to use "factory lean" to increase manufacturing throughput. Toyota now produces about $1 million output per employee per year—around four times the norm for auto companies. Maybe the stock buyers who believe Toyota is worth more than all other auto companies combined aren't so dumb.

Finally, let's turn to the trickiest measurement of all: speed.

Estimate value-creating time for developers

Ask your developers (anonymously, at least at first) what fraction of their time is spent creating value—creating useable new knowledge or manufacturing hardware. Calculate how much you could increase your throughput by increasing your fraction of value-adding creating time. Publicize.

Out-learning the competition

Everyone wants to go "faster" in development; but what does faster mean?

Speed should refer to the rate at which we learn. Conventional measures of speed, such as the time between project approval and manufacturing launch, can be actively destructive. Going to market twice as fast but learning half as much produces quality problems and doesn't gain on the competition. Unfortunately, learning is hard to measure, but here are some useful concepts.

First, you can directly measure the time required to answer a single question about a design: the time required to go from concept to model to simulation results, or from concept to prototype to test.

4. Cycle time from concept through simulation and test results.

Relentless attention to this instrument allowed one Delphi Rochester Technical Center fuel injector team to cut both times from weeks for simulation and months for test down to 24 hours each. They could get an idea in the morning, and have test or simulation results the next morning.

Reduce learning cycle time

Determine the basic learning cycle times for your organization. Set a target of reducing them by, say, 10% per quarter.

Similarly, Honda designs engines as a large-scale series of such learning cycles, designing, building, and testing a new engine every quarter. (This focus on rapid learning cycles drives new Honda suppliers crazy because Honda refuses to freeze specifications.) This is perhaps four times as fast as U.S. companies, so Honda can go through eight learning cycles to U.S. companies' three, and still be faster overall.

Second, you can directly assess how much you know, and how fast you are improving. Establish a breakdown of the kinds of things you need to know in a given product line. Start with the "integration, innovation, and feasibility" breakdown; later, you'll want more detailed and specific categories. Rate each category on a four-point scale, like a university grading system. The best way to assess your knowledge is to examine your trade-off sheets, but until you have trade-off sheets, you can just make a subjective assessment. Do this quarterly or monthly, and look at the change in your grade-point average.

5. Knowledge grade and rate of change.

The hardest part is being honest with yourself. Worse, at some point you'll have to change from a four-point scale, because you will have learned more than you would have dreamed possible when you started, and you'll realize how much more there still is to learn.

 Grade your company's ability to learn

> You guessed it. Grade your company's ability to learn within each phase of the product development process. Try to get information on a lean competitor's learning cycles and evaluate yourself competitively.

Said one U.S. engineer working at Toyota, "The real difference between Toyota and the U.S. companies I worked for is how much Toyota knows." Said another, "I'm not very experienced, but with this notebook [of trade-off curve sheets], I could design a pretty good auto body. Not as good as the experienced Toyota engineers though." And one more, in a U.S. company: "I've figured out the problem. We don't know what makes the difference between the product working and the product failing. We hired a retiree from a lean competitor. It's *amazing* what he knows."

Third, you can measure the time between product launches. This shorter this time is, the more often you get to sample the market, and the more you can learn. However, this is just the inverse of the throughput, which we discussed in the previous section. More throughput equals less time between launches. Further, this measure is so clouded by issues of the size of the project and the quality of the work, that I recommend you *don't* try to measure it.

Finally, you can assess the lead-time between a technical or market opportunity arising and satisfying the customer need with full-rate production of a quality product. Lead-time is critical because all competitors get access to new technical ideas and new market information at about the same time. You win if you are consistently faster than the competition at learning enough to achieve full-rate production at high quality, which allows feedback from the market and the production process.

6. Lead-time between technical or market opportunity and full-rate production of a winning product.

Lead-time is the sum of four periods:

- *Reaction time* between the opportunity appearing and the company deciding to invest.

- *Exploration time*, during which the team explores multiple alternative implementations (and knowledge-value is efficiently added).

- *Lock-in time*, during which only a single solution is detailed.

- *Fix-up time*, during which the company tries to deal with the problems with the solution.

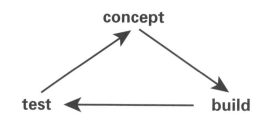

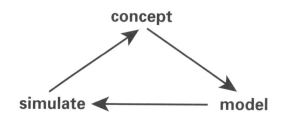

What can you learn from this?

You should spend your resources in the exploration phase. Only exploration efficiently adds knowledge. Lock-in and fix-up add knowledge only about the current solution. This doesn't help future projects, or do much about a bad initial concept in this one. Unfortunately, many companies do all their exploration during the "quote" process. Others explore using an advanced development process that is under funded and out of touch with market and manufacturing reality.

Don't separate a leisurely advanced development from a rushed product development. They contribute equally to lead time.

Try to make reaction time negative by starting the project before you've pinned down the opportunity. Opportunities normally arise at fairly predictable intervals, set by human ability to learn and change. For example, microprocessors double in speed every 18 months. Major changes in automotive buying tastes seem to happen about every eight years, with minor changes on about a four-year pace. Launch new projects to a cycle based on these time frames.

If you move to negative reaction times with regular, cyclic projects, you won't know what the change will be. So, you need to explore a variety of concepts, and you need to adjust your targets depending on what turns out to be technically feasible. This is the essence of set-based concurrent engineering (see Part 3). If you explore broadly enough, leaving yourself open to new concepts but testing them aggressively before committing to them, you can accept new concepts until quite late in development. Lock-in and fix-up periods will become very short.

FYI: Toyota's lead time

Toyota's basic lead-time is under two years, longer for totally new engine or manufacturing concepts, shorter for some simpler subsystems and smaller changes.

Here's how it works.

- Toyota's strong functional departments and suppliers are continually exploring new concepts, independent of any particular project.

- Vehicles are refreshed every four years. Toyota appoints a project leader and team (part time) about two years before launch.

- The basic style is determined 12 to 18 months before launch, but minor adjustments still are possible.

- Suppliers and departments provide multiple alternative concepts. Final decisions between some subsystem concepts might occur as late as six months before launch. Thus, almost all the development time is spent in exploration.

- By the final decision, the concept selected has been fairly thoroughly tested, so the lock-in time is short and the fix-up time almost non-existent. Ramp-up to full rate production is a negligible two weeks.

The auto industry doesn't publish lead-time statistics, but my guess is that Toyota is more than twice as fast as its American competitors. Experience with U.S. teams shows that a 30%-to-50% time reduction is feasible even the first time a team tries to use the lean methods; further reductions should be possible with increased experience and deeper implementation.

Going faster improves profitability in several ways:

- Saving time saves money. The size of a team is determined mostly by the range of expertise required. So, getting done faster frees resources.

- In markets with low switching costs for the customer to change from one supplier to another, going faster means you get your share of the market sooner. You probably keep it just as long, so you add some months or years of profit to your ROI.

- In markets with high switching costs, getting to market first could mean you get most of the market—and you get to keep it.

- If you are selling to industrial customers that are in a hurry themselves, the promise of speed may be enough by itself to radically improve market share and ROI.

- Above all, of course, going faster means learning faster. If you learn 20% faster than your competitors, 30 projects later you will be 60% ahead, a tremendous advantage.

That's it! Time to wrap up this Part.

 DO

Identify opportunities to reduce lead time

Assess and publicize your lead time, from opportunity to successful project. Compare with your strongest competitor's. Analyze where the time goes: Reaction time? Lock-in? Fix-up? Point out that these periods add much lower value than does exploration time, and start a debate on how to increase exploration time.

Summary: The learnings-to-costs-ratio

You can put all of your measurements together as the learning-to-costs ratio, which equals:

integration (especially customer) learning X innovation X feasibility learning

---

cost X time X risk

Use this primarily qualitatively, as a guide to moving in the right direction. Anything that increases our understanding of customers and other integration needs, or improves innovation, or enables us to understand more quickly what works and what doesn't, is good. Anything that reduces cost, time, and risk is good.

If you feel the need, you can quantify the ratio. Use your assigned grades above the line. Use your actual development costs, or 1 over the value-adding time fraction, for the cost. Use basic cycle time, or lead-time, or their product for time. Use the fraction of less than completely successful products, or the engineering teams' risk estimates, for risk.

So what did you learn in Part 1?

- The aim of development is to produce operational value streams. Development systems are good if they produce consistently profitable operational value streams.

- Value is created during development by building manufacturing equipment and by creating knowledge that understands customers, creates innovations to satisfying them, and wisely decides which innovations to use.

- Lean development methods produce better results and are more reliable, cheaper, and faster than conventional methods.

- You can estimate the effectiveness of your development programs using a variety of instruments. You can use the same instruments to help guide and improve development processes.

- You have to be careful not to "bend the needles" by rewarding individuals for good showings on the instruments.

It's time to dig deeper. Why do so many conventional development processes cost so much and perform so poorly? Because they waste knowledge. This is the subject of Part 2.

Part 2: Seeing Waste in Development

Why don't conventional development processes perform better? Why are there so many late, over-budget, or unprofitable projects? What happens to developers' 60% or more wasted time? Above all, how can you learn to clearly see what is wrong in your organization so that you can fix it?

This Part will help you learn to see wastes of knowledge. Seeing the waste will help you to:

- decide whether to change and what to change

- build the case for change

- identify things you can change immediately

- understand the lean system

- tailor the lean system to your situation

- continue to improve

You are in business to make money (or you are reading the wrong book). Seeing waste will allow you to quickly improve processes (and make more money) without a lot of complex analytical tools. You won't have to wait for black belts, big project efforts, or senior managers—though expert support, some major efforts, and commitment from the top are helpful. In Toyota plants, line operators improve each individual job— eliminate a waste—an average of once per week, with approval from supervisors.

Taiichi Ohno, sometimes called the father of the Toyota Production System (TPS), originally identified seven wastes in production (not development): overproduction, correction, movement of material, wasted human motion, waiting, inventory, and unnecessary processing.

His most important and counter-intuitive intellectual accomplishment was recognizing that over-production—making more than is needed right now—is the most important waste because it creates other wastes.

These wastes can be applied to any physical activity. For example, mopping floors is necessary nonvalue-creating work (not waste). Janitors can see waste by identifying the occupants of the office as customers. The janitors' output to these internal customers is a clean and comfortable office. Mopping creates value. Changing the water in the pail is nonvalue-creating but necessary. Wastes include walking further than necessary to change the water (wasted motion), mopping a clean floor (overproduction), skipping areas (defects), and mopping with dirty water (defects). Any janitor can think of ideas for eliminating these wastes without complex statistical or financial analysis.

Some development activities, such as prototype building and machine installation, are physical production activities, so we can apply Ohno's insights directly to them. We also can apply production waste concepts and production improvement concepts such as visual workplace controls.

Learn from lean manufacturing

If your company has people skilled in lean manufacturing, work with them to improve the operations of your labs and prototype shops.

However, the most important wastes in development are wastes of knowledge. Toyota has never formulated these: The ideas below are my abstraction from experience, logic, and many discussions with lean developers. In fact, no one in my more than 100 interviews with lean developers in the Toyota system ever mentioned the word waste. But they should have. The waste concept helps a lot in understanding their system.

To review, from the viewpoint of the ultimate customer, development is like floor mopping—a nonvalue-creating but necessary activity. Development's primary customer is operations. Development creates an operational value stream, from suppliers through factories into product features and out to customers. The difference between profitable and unprofitable operational value streams is how much usable knowledge is created and delivered by development. So, the primary wastes in development are connected with knowledge, not physical transformation.

The hard part of developing "eyes for waste" in development is that most waste is caused by "doing things right" within the conventional framework. The more well-versed you are in conventional development and management theory, the harder it is to see the waste. Remember the "unconscious incompetence, conscious incompetence, conscious competence, unconscious competence" learning model from the introduction (see Page 7). This part is designed to make you a lot more conscious of your incompetence. That probably will make you uncomfortable, and you may feel overwhelmed. Relax … Parts 3 and 4 will tell you what to do.

There are three primary categories of knowledge wastes; each has two additional associated categories. Each waste has an associated symbol to be used on *timeline maps* of development processes that we will use. Each waste is intuitive once we start thinking about knowledge as the primary value created from development—and each is a direct consequence of standard development practices.

The wastes frequently occur together, so that the same practice creates all three kinds of waste.

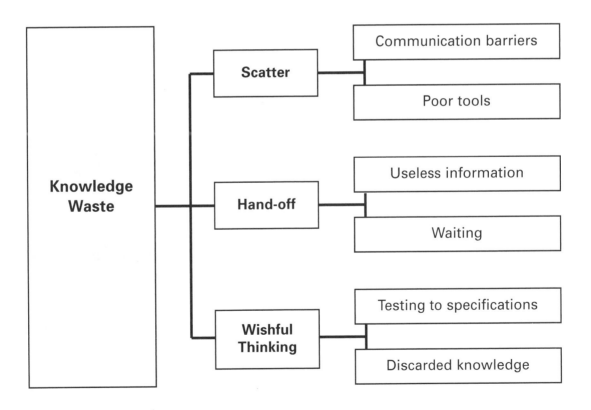

Scatter

Where does the time go? Why do we never seem to know what we need to know at the right time? Why do studies show that most engineers spend most of their time just trying to find information? Scatter.

We are all familiar with scatter—actions that make knowledge ineffective by disrupting its flow. Scatter basically disrupts the subtle interactions required for teamwork. Here are some common situations in development, and some conventional responses, and the ways they create scatter.

Scatter and its Consequences

	Situation	Conventional response	Scatter effect	Lean response
1	Things are going badly	Re-organize	Obsoletes interaction knowledge	Find root cause
2	The project is falling behind	Add more developers to the team	Disrupts communication	Supervisors pitch in
3	The purchasing agents are slow finding suppliers	Call them more often	Distracts purchasing	Find and fix root cause
4	We keep having product failures	Add more tasks and checks to the development process	Distracts developers	Find and fix root cause
5	The customer wants something new	Add a rush development project	Overloads resources, produces new failures	Steady drumbeat of innovation
6	We're having problems with the manufacturing system	Keep the manufacturing engineers on the project until the system is running properly	Manufacturing engineers not available for next project; problem repeats	Set-based concurrent engineering, rotation of people from plant on to the team.

A little more detail:

1. Reorganization requires people to learn the specifics of their new job. More importantly, it makes them relearn the network of communications, understand how their components fit into the system, and recreate the real process of working together—which is always different from the official process. For a while, no one knows who to talk to. (Of course, organizational changes are sometimes needed. But conventional organizations overestimate their benefits and underestimate their costs because they do not recognize their disruptive effect on knowledge flow.)

2. Adding more developers to a team usually slows things down because the new developers don't speak the team's language.

3. Harassing people to get a faster response works—for the harasser. For everyone else, response gets much slower because dropping one job to address another reduces efficiency. Workload fluctuations and demands for rapid response (i.e., unplanned switching among activities, reprioritization) cause organizational and personal disruption. Materials wind up in the wrong place; ideas and data get lost; people feel angry and exhausted all the time.

4. Adding more work to already overloaded developers just means that more things fall through the cracks.

5. Adding projects at random intervals causes major fluctuations in the working environment. The request for knowledge that worked last time fails this time, so workers have to chase after the knowledge. Juggling priorities, expediting, and following up demand more and more of the day. Total throughput declines —and, because the organization is falling behind its competitors, demands to add more projects increase.

6. Keeping manufacturing engineers on projects after launch means that they are not available for the next project—and it, too, will suffer from faulty manufacturing systems.

Scatter often is a death spiral, a feedback loop that makes things worse and worse. As things "fall through the cracks" because of disorganization, developers spend more time "fighting fires," responding to demands for information by others, and looking for information and harassing other developers to try to get action. Everything becomes a crisis. Since nothing goes according to plan, senior managers try to gain control by reorganizing, imposing arbitrary rules, demanding more reports, more tasks, and immediate explanations of problems. Since nothing is stable long enough for good feedback on actual contributions, people have to spend more and more of their time doing things to look good—making more elaborate presentations and generating more elaborate ideas for solving the problem. Worst of all, the people who are most successful in this chaotic environment naturally rise to positions of power—where they encourage the organization to behave in the ways that made them successful. In these ways, the responses to scatter create more scatter.

The big problem is loss of the subtle interactions that actually make machines and companies successful. Most individual engineering tasks are relatively straightforward. Anyone with sound basic engineering qualifications can read a book (or a trade-off curve sheet) and do them. But people new to a position don't understand the subtle human and technical interactions of the total system and have difficulty contributing to its integration. For example, members of the Abrams M1 tank design team told me that only two engineers involved had ever worked on a tank design. Nonetheless, each subsystem of the tank is a technological marvel. Abrams is the fastest, best-armored, most lethal tank in the world. But it is a questionable system, too heavy for easy deployment, subject to frequent and expensive breakdowns, and consuming incredible quantities of fuel.

Stop increasing the scatter

Much scatter is caused by direct management action, and you can reduce it right now by doing nothing! For example:

- Stop reorganizing.

- Reduce demands for information on short notice from subordinates.

- Respond to "fires" with the least disruptive but effective response. If it is someone's job to put out the fire, let them do it.

- Stop sending out or replying to excessive e-mail or voice mail.

- Think twice about adding more projects.

- Stop adding formal structure (i.e., tasks, checks, reports) to your development process.

Usually, a fundamental cause of scatter is conventional management assumptions that we can create organizational structure (order) through procedure manuals, organization charts, and directives. In fact, order has to emerge from the interactions among the people, which takes time.

Scatter has two important associated wastes: barriers to communication and the use of inappropriate tools.

Barriers to Communication

Barriers to communication directly prevent the flow of knowledge.

They include:

- *Physical barriers* such as distance, incompatible computer formats, etc.
- *Social barriers* such as the corporate "class systems" and management behaviors that prevent communication.
- *Skill barriers* such as people not knowing how to turn data into usable knowledge.
- *Information channels*.

In more detail:

Physical barriers start with incompatible computer formats, the most obvious barrier with the most technical fixes and no permanent ones, at least until the industry's commitment to open standards becomes real. We might as well lump differences in human languages along with sheer physical distance. Many companies now are exacerbating both problems by moving development overseas in pursuit of lower engineering labor costs.

Social barriers cause most companies to waste the expertise of machinists, technicians, and production operators because people with university degrees don't know how to listen to them. (I used to annoy my fellow faculty members by saying that many of my discussions with university professors taught me nothing, but I never visited a machine shop without learning something.) Formal rules or informal attitudes keep engineers out of the shop or plant; and operators and machinists out of engineering. Similarly, the best engineers in many companies are siphoned off to move paper, sit in meetings, and relay information from working engineers because they are now "managers," not "engineers." Their knowledge decays rapidly. And many companies punish reporting bad news, so people don't. "Not invented here" syndrome often prevents knowledge from getting in from outside.

Often, mechanical engineers *lack skills* or tools for describing geometry, so they explain geometry to CAD operators in English. They don't know how to put knowledge into simple written and graphical form, so meetings multiply.

Information flows through *channels*, on paper. This leftover from the days of typewriters and carbon paper produces multiple, late, and conflicting copies of the same data.

Start breaking down the barriers to communication

Ask any cross-functional group of developers, *"What stops us from getting the right knowledge to the right place at the right time?"* You'll get more ideas than you want. Implement the quick and simple solutions, but report back to the group whether or not you take action.

To reduce distance barriers, design and build where your customers are. To reduce social barriers, have everyone work in the plant for one day per quarter. Teach engineers to sketch, and provide CAD systems that are tools, not careers. Replace channeled information flow with electronic knowledge bases people can draw from as needed.

Poor Tools

Why do the companies with the most carefully detailed development processes have the most trouble? It's partly because the written processes *require* developers to use inefficient techniques.

We need some root cause analysis here. After all, these processes often are defined by skilled developers, and most steps are included to prevent some disaster from reoccurring. So why are developers overwhelmed by detail, while managers complain bitterly that problems keep arising?

That's why the Toyota developers kept saying "case by case" whenever I tried to pin them down on a standard process. They designed out known problems using knowledge captured in the trade-off curve sheets discussed in Part 3, while anticipating new problems and developing appropriate new analysis and tests. Toyota standardizes minimum expected knowledge (and then demands that people keep learning).

Conventional companies find that "to the developer with only a hammer, everything looks like a nail." More problems; more standard tasks. Soon, people cut corners, copying old failure modes and effects analysis, using finite element models only to get a strength number rather than to really understand the stress distribution, fudging the business case. More failures. Management becomes frustrated and demands more crosschecks, reports, and tasks. Developers become more overwhelmed. The development process has entered a death spiral: the more they "improve" the process, the worse the failures.

Next, conventional companies try to eliminate tasks from the process. Catastrophe often follows because the tasks had been added for a reason. For example, NASA's "cheaper, smaller, better" initiatives led to a series of dramatic failures.

So, what are the effective, lean countermeasures? How can you achieve a disciplined, effective process while allowing (indeed, requiring) developers to decide case by case on the most efficient means available to create knowledge?

In the long run, you will want to adopt some key lean development elements:

- Establish clear responsibilities for results, not process following. Establish flow and pull management. Then you can afford to let your elaborate processes die to the cheers of the developers.

- Teach developers how to turn data into usable knowledge—the trade-off curve sheets discussed in Part 3. Require them to design to prevent problems rather than simulating or testing in order to discover problems.

- Teach standardization through value focus—the basic rule that says that everyone is responsible for doing things the way that works.

In the meantime, use the flowchart on Page 39 to mine your procedures for useful information while encouraging developers to take responsibility for using the best tool to get the needed information. As an example, we'll use the flow chart to analyze and improve a standard tool in conventional development, Failure Modes and Effects Analysis (FMEA).

FYI: Analyzing tools for waste: an FMEA example

We begin at the top left: FMEA answers the following questions:

1. *How can the product or process fail?*
2. *What is the probability of each failure?*
3. *How serious are the consequences?*
4. *What is the plan to prevent or to detect possible failure?*
5. *(In some companies) does the product of the failure probabilities and consequences fall below a critical risk level? If not, the team "fails the gate review."*

Does answering these questions add usable knowledge? Yes, for 1 through 4. But question 5, used to evaluate the team's performance, seems more likely to "bend the needle" and destroy useful information.

Moving right on the "no" arrow, we realize this question was intended to reassure management that the product or process is safe. Management needs to learn to assess the safety of the product more directly by looking at the parts and performance data and asking engineers how they have assured themselves on safety.

Are questions 1 through 4 the most important questions? No. 1 clearly is. But the probability and exact consequences of failure are important only if we design for failure! The more important questions are:

What causes the failure?
Under what circumstances will the product fail?
What design circumstances will prevent failure?

These questions lead to designs that find a better way and won't fail. They also are much easier to answer accurately because estimating probabilities of failure is very difficult, in part because the probability is so low for a well-designed product. Murphy's law is easier and safer—anything that can go wrong, will go wrong—so design so things can't go wrong!

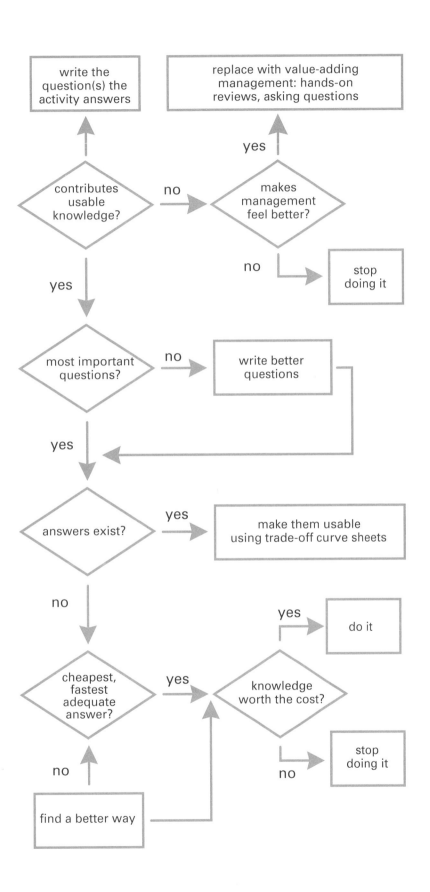

Start eliminating waste

Get started eliminating wasteful steps and tools in your development process by holding workshops and using the flowchart. This is a good way to help your designers focus on the knowledge to be gained, rather than the tasks to be checked off. You'll see immediate benefits and start increasing confidence in lean.

Toyota makes little use of formal FMEA. Instead, it builds its development process around trade-off sheets that answer the questions we defined. You can use the same analysis process to identify and eliminate poor tool waste throughout your process.

I hope you are beginning to see that scatter and its associated wastes—barriers to communication and the use of poor tools—result from "doing things right" using conventional thinking. You'll see the same when we move on to additional wastes. First, we need to introduce another tool—one that can help you to visualize waste in your system.

Timeline maps help see the wastes

How can you "see" the development process? (Seeing is important, because about half of your brain is devoted to processing visual information. You understand better visually.) The better you see the process, the better you'll find wastes.

I recommend using resource consumption timelines such as this one for a typical complete development process. You also can do timeline maps for parts of a process, such as a prototype build.

The horizontal axis represents project time before (and a little after) launch, or some other convenient target date or time. Use any convenient units, from hours to years. The vertical axis represents effort. Typically, the units here are full-time equivalents (FTE). Two people each working 1/2 time on the project is one FTE.

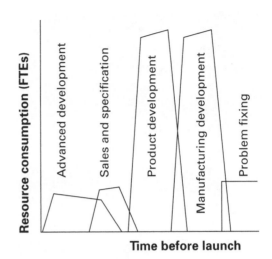

Can you see the scatter resulting from changes in workload? Different parts of the organization see big peaks in the effort they apply to the project. This means that they have to try to schedule their work across many projects, and if one project gets out of sync, the disruption can be enormous. You can show this by putting a scatter symbol on the timeline wherever there is a radical change in workload.

If you already have pictures of your processes using some kind of box-and-arrow chart (i.e., a critical path method chart, a process flow diagram, or a factory-type value-stream chart) use them to analyze the wastes in your current system. However, you need to understand the problems associated with them:

- They don't show resource loads and therefore can't help to achieve level loading or resource planning.

- They force sequential thinking—this comes before that—which does not reflect the way development actually operates. In fact, sequential thinking is what we are trying to eliminate.

- They force channeled thinking—this person communicates with that person—which we also want to get rid of (in favor of a pull system, in which knowledge is universally available).

As we eliminate wastes and move to a lean development system, sequential processes become parallel. Parallel processes run more smoothly, are easier to coordinate with other processes, and result in far more efficient multi-way communication.

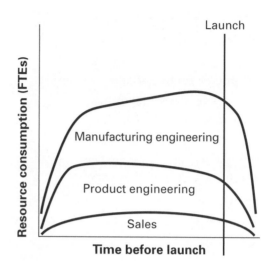

 DO

Map your processes and identify wastes

You can map:
- An example project.
- A generic process for a family of products.
- A part of a process, such as an engineering change process, or a "model-and-simulate" process.

Draw a timeline map for some process you know. Small-scale processes such as engineering changes often involve a lot of scatter in the form of channeled knowledge flow, etc. Mark it on the map. Keep marking your map as you learn more wastes, especially hand-off, waiting, and wishful thinking.

Later, mark up other maps. Hang them in many departments; publicize them; use them to agitate for change.

Hand-Off

It is time to look deeper. What is the most fundamental waste in conventional companies? Hand-off.

A hand-off occurs whenever we separate *knowledge*, *responsibility*, *action*, and *feedback*. Hand-off is a disaster because it results in decisions being made by people who do not have enough knowledge to make them well or the opportunity to make them happen.

For example, in your company, who is responsible for making money for each project? Do they have the knowledge required? Will they do the work? Will they get effective feedback from the market?

In many companies, only the president actually is responsible for making money from development projects. Salespeople establish specifications, engineering tries to meet them, the project leader administers the project, the functional department heads provide guidance—but only the CEO is responsible for profit.

But the president doesn't understand the technical details of the project and isn't going to do the work that will determine project success. Nor will he be involved enough to learn effectively from experience with the product in manufacturing and marketing. These companies separate *knowledge*, *responsibility*, *action*, and *feedback*. They build in hand-off.

hand-off

Contrast this with my role as president, owner, and chief engineer of a small specialty machine company. I was responsible to the customer for success (in fact, my house was on the line). I was not an expert in every aspect of the business, by any means, but I knew enough about all the aspects—and about the principles of system design—to integrate the pieces into effective systems. I did the system design, including picking people to design the subsystems. I tested the machines and watched the customer use them—a feedback process from which I learned a lot. There was no hand-off.

Why is hand-off so destructive? Because the best teachers on their best days get across less than 30% of their knowledge. So, hand-off implies throwing away at least 70% of knowledge on its way to the people doing the work. Worse, those conventionally responsible for the most critical decisions usually are too busy to get even 10% of the knowledge. And, generally, no one gets a chance to really learn very much because personnel turbulence and the diffusion of responsibility prevent effective feedback.

FYI: Combining knowledge, responsibility, action, and feedback in the U.S. Army

When I was a new infantry second lieutenant in 1973, the Army taught me a lot of management theory in a classroom at Fort Benning. I would have authority over the 40 men in my platoon, and I learned how to motivate them using my authority to reward and punish, as well as psychological theory.

Fortunately, as the lessons of defeat in Vietnam sank in over the next few years, the Army changed. Some figured it out: Soldiers will follow a leader who knows how to accomplish the mission while keeping alive as many men as possible. So what does an infantry platoon leader need to know? How to shoot (so he can teach shooting and protect himself); how to read a map; how to look at land and see where it protects his men from the enemy's bullets, and where it allows them to fire at the enemy. And these skills can be learned only in the field, where mistakes are instantly visible. In short, the platoon leader needs to combine knowledge, responsibility, action, and feedback—and if he does, he can stop worrying about authority.

Some more examples of hand-off:

- Holding project leaders responsible for meeting specifications defined by someone else.

- Moving people in and out of development rather than assigning them from beginning to end.

- Dividing engineering design among release engineers, CAD operators, and analysts.

- Holding manufacturing engineers responsible for making new products without teaching them how to constrain the product engineers for manufacturability.

Why does this happen? Because it is the essence of scientific management:

- One person (the manager) decides what to do (responsibility).

- Another person (the expert) defines the process and rules for doing it (knowledge).

- A third person (the operator) does it (action).

- It will be done the same way (the "one best way") forever—no feedback.

Scientific management is designed to create hand-off situations. So is the basic tool most companies use to plan and control development—the critical path chart. It is built around "tasks" that the developers must accomplish. This means the developers are responsible for accomplishing the tasks instead of making money. It connects the tasks using dependency arrows—points at which responsibility is transferred from one developer to another.

We can mark up our development chart with hand-off:

- A hand-off after advanced development because advanced development selects the concept, which then must be executed by product development.

- A hand-off between sales and specification and product development, because the product development organization must implement the specifications decided by the proposal team.

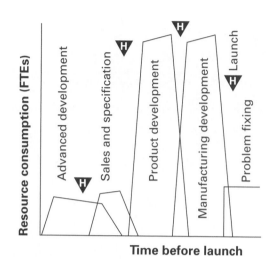

- A hand-off between product development and manufacturing development, because manufacturing engineering must implement the design determined by product development.

- A hand-off between manufacturing development and the plant, which must use the system designed by manufacturing engineering.

Hand-off creates a death spiral indeed; the mother of all the death spirals in conventional companies. Once scientific management has done the initial damage, people begin actively avoiding responsibility and knowledge. And why not? Why bother to learn when you will not have the opportunity to put the knowledge to work and take responsibility (and credit) for the results? And who would want responsibility without the knowledge and ability to take action to carry it out? Only someone desperate for authority, which conventional theory aligns with responsibility. But in fact, authority doesn't enable us to carry out a responsibility; only knowledge, action, and feedback can do that.

Thus, hand-offs create finger-pointing—the conventional management salute. Blame management—demands for explanations of problems, efforts to redefine problems so they are someone else's responsibility, and reports, reports, reports—can become the primary activity of middle managers. (One big payoff of lean development for middle managers is an end to the blame game.) Those best at playing these games rise to the top and perpetuate the process. Many companies die from this disease.

 Fight hand-off

You'll be fighting hand-off as long as you pursue lean development. For now, spread awareness of the problem. Post a definition in the hallway. Mark hand-off waste in red on a development map (either a timeline or an existing box-and-arrow chart) and post it. Go through the list below and check the box if your company suffers from the waste. Add your own examples. Post that, too.

✓ Different people define part geometry, analyze, and make decisions. Manufacturing engineering doesn't effectively constrain product design.

✓ Project leaders are not responsible for profit and system design, which is the biggest influence on profit.

✓ Functional department managers are not held responsible for supporting project leaders.

✓ The personnel records system doesn't track demonstrated skill, the projects that developers work on, their contributions to the projects, and project success.

✓ The plant doesn't provide people to the development team well before launch.

✓ A staff group defines and enforces the development process.

✓ "Advanced development" picks the basic concept, and product engineering carries it into production.

✓ Sales, senior managers, or a quote team take contracts, which the project leader and team must execute.

✓ Managers make decisions for the development team (such as, what specifications to pursue).

Useless Information

Where does the time go? Why do developers spend only 20% of their time adding value?

A lot of time goes to chasing useful information because of scatter. A lot more goes to generating, chasing, and receiving useless information because of hand-offs.

Information is useless if it doesn't help understand the customer or other integration issues, doesn't innovate, and doesn't provide a basis for good decisions. It doesn't improve the operational value stream. It is created because someone wants it.

Hand-offs cause the generation of useless information. Developers have the knowledge and do the work. Managers have responsibility and demand information to maintain the illusion of control. Problems arise, and managers demand more information. Much development work therefore goes into generating information solely to reassure or impress a manager, or avoid or assign blame.

Examples:

- Most PowerPoint-style presentations.

- Progress reports in which developers solemnly swear they are on schedule.

- Failure mode and effects analysis that are completed pro forma, without generating new knowledge.

Some useless information is generated because the person doing the work feels like it and isn't responsible for profitability. Examples:

- The endless optimization some engineers like to engage in, leading to the saying "shoot the engineers and launch the product."

- The creation of a new design that is not more profitable than the old. (An actual case manager: "Why did you design a new control circuit when the old one met the customer's requirements?" Engineer: "I already designed the old one.")

Reduce the waste of useless information

The first steps are easy. Just:

- Ask working developers what useless information they are being required to create.

- Apply the flowchart discussed under waste of scatter to eliminate or replace the information demand.

- Introduce the new management concepts and system to really do what all those reports were supposed to do—the hard part.

Waiting

Most companies have, at one time or another, had a product line get into so much trouble that they had to go a lot faster than normal. So they put together a capable team, relieved its members of other responsibilities, told them not to worry about following the standard process, and moved them into the same location; and sure enough, the team went twice as fast as normal. But these companies found that they can't replicate the process. As soon as they re-impose the standard process, things slow way down. Yet we know that Toyota does follow a standard (if simple) process, does not co-locate or dedicate developers to a single project; and yet goes twice as fast on every project. Why?

Because the standard conventional methods of planning, organizing, and controlling projects—PERT, the critical path method (even when modified to a "critical chain" method) and phase gates—cause the waste of waiting. Sequence—finish this before starting that—is their whole point! No wonder a decade of repeating the concurrent engineering mantra did most companies relatively little good. The tools worked against the goal.

But sequence doesn't make sense in development! It's hard to find a development upstream process that has to finish before a downstream process can start. (The downstream process often can't finish before the upstream process, but so what?) This is a major difference between development and manufacturing, and between development and construction, the environment for which PERT was designed.

Sequencing creates a batch process in which all the decisions and learning of a particular kind happen at once. This:

- Slows the process because people wait longer than they need to before starting.

- Creates one-way rather than multi-way information flows: The upstream processes don't get enough input from the downstream processes.

- Gives the upstream developers more power than the downstream, creating quality problems.

- Causes large variations in workload, which in turn causes scatter waste.

Specification ▶ **System design** ▶ **Part design** ▶ **Manufacturing design**

For example:

- Engineering waits for specifications before beginning to design. Inevitably, the specifications are unrealistic. They either push the design too hard and create cost and quality problems; or they fail to take advantage of opportunities that emerge once design is underway.

- Manufacturing engineering waits for a product design before beginning production system design. The product therefore has to be designed based on the characteristics of the old manufacturing system—to the extent it is designed for manufacture at all—preventing joint innovation and optimization of the combined product and manufacturing system.

- Plants wait for manufacturing engineering to demonstrate the manufacturing system before becoming involved.

- Suppliers are chosen late in the process—preventing joint innovation and optimization of the product, subsystems, and suppliers' manufacturing systems.

Some companies try to use schedules to manage the wildly varying workloads; some don't even try. The schedules are obsolete before the ink is dry. Development has too many uncertainties, and so batching produces terrible resource conflicts.

We will see later that lean development concepts (i.e., set-based concurrent engineering and pull/flow planning) allow a much greater degree of concurrency, multi-directional information flow, and leveled resource demands.

 Reduce the waste of waiting

Get started. Hold cross-functional workshops. Ask people what they do. Plot the information in a timeline. Ask them why they wait.

Unfortunately, the real answer almost always is *"because I'm really busy, and this isn't a crisis yet."* You will need the tools of pull, flow, and cadence to take your company out of crisis mode.

Wishful Thinking

So far, we've looked at the wastes that cause most of the loss of value-adding time—wastes of scatter and hand-off. These wastes also cause many defective projects. Scatter causes defects because the right knowledge doesn't get to right place. Hand-off causes defects because the people making the decisions and doing the work don't have the required knowledge. But there is another major source of defects. Why do most projects run over budget and over schedule? Why do most companies have so much trouble during manufacturing ramp up to full-rate production?

Because of the waste of wishful thinking.

Wishful thinking means making decisions without data or operating blindly. Conventional development concepts require wishful thinking.

Conventional development begins with a specification. But every specification is a compromise between what customers really want and what nature allows. At the beginning of the project customers don't know what they want, and developers don't know what nature allows, except on the basis of old data. Setting specifications at the beginning of a project is wishful thinking, which often produces market misses, excessive cost, or serious quality problems.

Pictured below is a conventional process as drawn by my favorite professor at MIT. The process rapidly selects a single design concept, details it, attempts to prove it will work, and modifies it when it doesn't. This means that the most critical decision of the project—selecting the basic concept—has to be made without much data.

The team may never find out whether the concept chosen was best; it finds out whether it is good enough only at the end of the project. Often, it isn't, and then the team scrambles to try other alternatives under the worst possible circumstances: raising costs, compromising quality, and running over schedule.

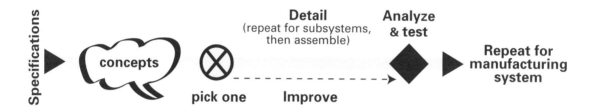

"Waterfall" and "V" development processes first design the system, freezing the interfaces between the subsystems, then design subsystems. This allows independent subsystem designs, but also means that critical system decisions about the interfaces are made on the basis of old data about what is possible.

The resulting designs usually are distorted, pushing some subsystems too hard and others not hard enough. They usually allow little reuse of parts or manufacturing systems.

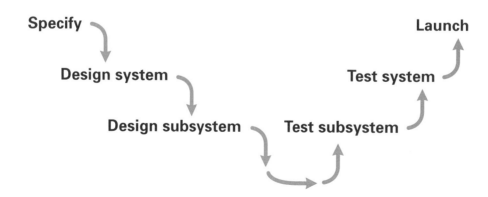

Many conventional companies select suppliers by a bid process. This requires publishing specifications, if not drawings, first. Thus, there is no opportunity to find out what suppliers can actually do, and therefore what system design and part specifications actually make sense. It also makes the selection on the basis of a promise—the quote. In my experience, relying on promises is wishful thinking. If the supplier is losing money, they find a way out, often by exploiting changes to renegotiate the contract.

Human beings dislike uncertainty, and often make decisions prematurely to reduce the uncertainty. A senior manager at Toyota said, "My job is to keep people from making decisions too quickly." Further, the natural intuition is that looking at one alternative is cheaper, easier, and faster than looking at multiple alternatives. This is usually wrong, because looking at a lot of alternatives early is usually cheaper than looking at a few alternatives later. But many people are hard to convince: "There is never time to do it right; always time to do it over."

On our timeline map, we see:

- Advanced development selects a fundamental development concept before there is proof that it will be profitable.
- Sales accepts a customer specification before there is evidence that it will be achievable.
- Product development selects a design before there is current evidence that it is manufacturable.

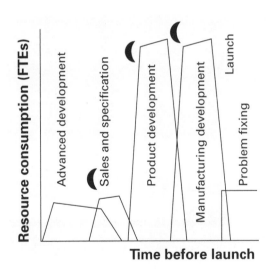

DO **Attack wishful thinking**

Mark up your process map with wishful thinking, and post it in the hall.

Whenever someone tells you that a problem is caused by X, ask, *"What alternative causes have you considered, and what data did you gather to rule them out?"*

Whenever someone says, *"I'm going to do A,"* ask, *"What alternative courses of action did you consider, and what data did you gather to rule them out?"*

Analyze past defective projects. Try to estimate the cost to the company of wishful thinking. Publicize.

As soon as possible, implement set-based concurrent engineering and training in "problem-solving sheets," discussed in Part 3.

Testing to Specifications

Why do you test your products during development? To make sure they are ready for the market, that they meet specifications?

This is standard, conventional practice. It's also wishful thinking. Testing to specifications cannot show that a product is ready for the market. Why? Statistically it is impossible to test enough to be confident of satisfying the modern demand for quality. One failure in 10,000 often can doom a product, but you cannot test 10,000 samples against every possible failure mode. Designs can pass tests to specifications and be ready to fall off a cliff.

Lean companies test primarily to find out the point of failure—and design to stay away from the failure. The failure points are recorded in trade-off curves, and these guide the design.

- This dramatically reduces costs. Toyota builds 70% to 90% fewer prototypes than do U.S. competitors, even though Toyota generally lags behind the U.S. in computer simulation capabilities. For example, Toyota does not do life tests on prototype vehicles; the trade-off curves can be refined just as well using production vehicles for the life tests, and the vehicles have already been designed for adequate life.[8]

8. This was the author's understanding at the time of writing.

Testing to specifications reduces the effectiveness of the test organization. A Ford team built a control system for door hardware (locks, window regulators, and mirror adjustments), which was to be used by both Ford and Mazda. The system went through three weeks of the Ford standard tests, which found 15 bugs. Mazda sent a test engineer who ignored the test procedures, tested aggressively, and found 30 more bugs in three days.

Testing's job is to break the product, record how it breaks, and advise Design Engineering on how to make it harder to break. Test engineers need to be independent, creative, and aggressive. Allowing Product Engineering to define the tests is like putting the fox in charge of the hen house.

 Test aggressively

Teach your test department to find and record the limits of performance and to provide recommendations for improvement. If customers require testing to specifications, fine, test up to the spec, and then go on to break the part.

Discarded Knowledge

Finally, what do you do after manufacturing launch with the knowledge you acquired during development?

Most companies file it and forget it, throwing away their most precious asset. There are several reasons:

- Conventional teams (and their supervisors) focus on getting the product out; capturing knowledge is way down on the priority list.

- Tests to specifications don't tell us much that can be useful next time.

- Above all, few engineers know how to turn data into useable knowledge.

 DO

Estimate current discarded knowledge

Try to estimate the cost of discarded knowledge. What fraction of engineers' time is spent trying to find knowledge that has already been developed at least once? Publicize.

Teach the use of the trade-off curve sheets discussed in Part 3. Make frequent inspection trade-off curve sheets a high priority for all departmental leaders.

Lessons learned so far

So what have you learned to do? In Part 1 you learned how to evaluate the performance of your development system by looking at project ROI; the rate of defective projects; the fraction of developer time that is spent adding value; and the rate of learning, including the time from opportunity to successful product.

In Part 2 you learned how to look for the root causes of poor performance in the form of wastes:

1) Scatter: management actions such as reorganization and workload variation that make knowledge hard to get to the right place; barriers to communication, such as the use of multiple paper forms to carry information through channels; and poor tools, which most often generate information that would have been useful in preventing a past problem but doesn't prevent future problems efficiently.

2) Hand-off: the most critical waste, occurring whenever a company separates responsibility, knowledge, action, and feedback; useless information, usually generated to provide management with the illusion of control; and waiting, the practice of putting developing learning into batches so that knowledge flows only one direction.

3) Wishful Thinking: making decisions without data; testing to specifications, which leaves the product vulnerable to problems too infrequent for the specifications to catch; and discarded knowledge, which is the failure to put everything learned during a project into usable form.

You learned to see the causes of these wastes in conventional management practices, particularly scientific management and the use of box-and-arrow methods to plan and control projects. You learned how to map your process to make the wastes more visible.

And you have a long list of things to do. Most of these items are intended to give your company a clearer picture of its current state—where it is now. I can't over-emphasize how important this is. One person can change an entire organization by holding up a mirror for the organization to accurately see itself. Try to be politically savvy. Try to be tactful. But be clear, forceful, and aggressive. Take every opportunity to refine and communicate your picture of what is happening.

You will build dissatisfaction with the current situation, as people see how much waste there is, and how poorly the company is performing compared with its potential. This dissatisfaction will combine with a vision of the future to pull your company forward.

So work on your to-do list. Get started motivating your company to change. And get on with the next part, which will help you form a vision of where you want to go.

Part 3: Seeing the Future: The Lean Development System

Overview

It's time for the fun stuff: How do we reduce the wastes in development? What would a good system look like?

This Part will help you to form a mental picture of the development system you want to have. You, with your colleagues, are going to create a new way of thinking and acting—even of feeling. Like artists, composers, carpenters, and plumbers, you will need a picture in your mind of what you are trying to create. It doesn't have to be perfect—just clear enough that you can tell whether you are going in the right direction, and clear enough to get you excited. This actually is a principle of lean development—your excitement about what you are trying to create pulls the team forward.

Emergent Learning

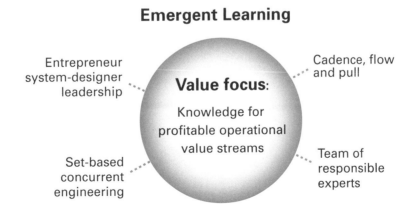

Entrepreneur system-designer leadership

Cadence, flow and pull

Value focus:

Knowledge for profitable operational value streams

Set-based concurrent engineering

Team of responsible experts

The lean development system, as practiced by Toyota and its suppliers and pictured here, can be summarized by the following principles, each of which is counter-intuitive in conventional practice.

- **Focus on creating knowledge and hardware for consistently profitable operational value streams.** (Manufacturing is the primary customer for development; knowledge is its primary value.) This principle *pulls* the rest of the system.

- **Embody this focus in *entrepreneur system designers* (ESDs)**—project (and possibly business line) leaders who are responsible for creating these profitable value streams. (Functional managers have only one job: supporting these ESDs!)

- **Support ESDs with *set-based concurrent engineering* (SBCE)** to eliminate risk while achieving high innovation and rapid learning by looking at multiple alternatives at every level of the system. (Spend money on more alternatives than you will use!)

- **Support SBCE with cadenced flow and pull project management** to minimize load variation and sequencing, and to get everyone to plan their own work. (Say goodbye to Microsoft Project and other critical path management tools.)

- **Support flow and pull management with teams of responsible experts** who design their own work, learn from conflict, and both create and use new knowledge. (A whole new job for management—supporting learning, rather than telling people what to do.)

As we discussed in the Introduction, a fundamental concept underlies the whole system: Useful order emerges from the whole organization learning how to fit things together. Useful order cannot be created efficiently by giving commands! Conventional development is designed to maximize the effectiveness of commands. Lean development is designed to maximize the efficiency of emergent learning.

As shown in this table, each element of the lean product development system provides specific countermeasures to the wastes discussed in Part 2. For example, the *entrepreneur system designer* and *team of responsible experts* counteract *hand-off waste* by putting responsibility, knowledge, action, and feedback together (i.e., "total responsibility").

That's the preview. Now, let's look at each element of the system in detail.

Countermeasures That the Five Principles Provide Against Product Development Waste

Wastes	Lean Product Development Principles				
	Value Focus: Knowledge & Operational Value Stream	**Entrepreneur System Designer**	**Set-Based Concurrent Engineering**	**Cadence, Flow & Pull**	**Teams of Responsible Experts**
Scatter	Clear Goals	Value-stream Focus	Reduced Uncertainty	Smoothed Workload	Self-Adjustment
Communication Barriers	Blurred boundaries	Cross-boundary translation	Two-way negotiation	Broad knowledge flow	Pull needed knowledge
Poor Tools	Procedures subservient to goals	Results needed	Simple, effective tools needed	Flexibility created	Experts design own work
Hand-off	System Focus	Total Responsibility		Planning and Action Together	Total Responsibility
Useless Information	Defined utility	Hands-on leadership		Simple controls	Self-discipline and peer feedback
Waiting for Knowledge	Incentives to act	Push for action	Concurrency enabled	Concurrent processes	Pull needed knowledge
Wishful Thinking	Excuses not Permitted	Success Required	Knowledge Precedes Decisions	Fast Learning Cycles	Responsible for Decisions Made
Testing to Specifications	Clear evaluation goals	Knowledge needed	Aggressive evaluation	Continuous Evaluation	"Red team"
Discarded Knowledge	Knowledge valued	Knowledge needed	Trade-off curves	Continuous learning	Knowledge built for future work

Impact of the Five Principles on High-level Product Development Measures

Measures	Lean Product Development Principles				
	Value Focus: Knowledge & Operational Value Stream	**Entrepreneur System Designer**	**Set-Based Concurrent Engineering**	**Cadence, Flow & Pull**	**Teams of Responsible Experts**
Better Functionality	Focus	Vision	Innovation & optimization	Rapid process improvement	Expertise and responsibility
More Reliable	Focus	Good decisions	Very low risk	Early evaluations	Expertise and responsibility
Cheaper	Focus	Cross-functional flow	No late failures	Minimal time wasted	Expertise and responsibility
Faster	Focus	Quick decisions	No late failures	Quick response	Quick response

Focusing on creating value

"Focusing on creating value"—who could argue with that? But what does it mean?

Development

Profitable Operational Value Stream

Lean development focuses on creating *usable* knowledge and equipment—knowledge and equipment that contribute to consistently profitable operational value streams.

Operational value streams—the output of development—run from suppliers through plants into product features and out to customers. Every link in this chain is critical. A "good" product and a bad manufacturing system, weak supplier, or unhappy customer represents a failed project.

(*"What,"* you may ask, *"about my huge prototype shop that spends 95% of its effort making prototypes for customers?"* O.K. Perhaps you make some money from the shop. But the real value lies in what you and your customer learn.)

For success—for consistently profitable operational value streams—we must know:

- What customers want and how to integrate our product into the legal, physical, and supplier environment.

- Our own manufacturing and development capabilities and how they can be used to provide customers' desires—and to beat the competition.

- The physics and aesthetics of our products.

- The capabilities and limitations of our suppliers and how these can be best integrated into our own system.

Above all, we must create improved system concepts for fitting all of these things together to make better operational value streams. Creating value means learning about the complete value stream—the complete system. Let's look at learning and then at the value stream.

The fundamental value-creating cycle

What is learning? How do we add value? We'll look at this question in many different ways. After all, that's what the whole book is about—but let's start here with the simplest —this figure.

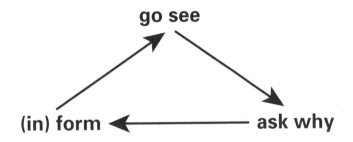

To create new knowledge, we must first "go see" something. "Go see" is an active, not a passive, process—an experiment, a mathematical derivation, or just a walk through a factory or a talk with a customer.

Once we see, we "ask why." What is the cause of what we see? What laws govern it?

Finally, the funny writing of "(in)form" is a pun. Often we "form" the understanding we acquire into something usable—a drawing, a prototype, an equation, a report, a procedure, a machine. Often we "inform" others.

Everything we will discuss—the entire machinery of lean development—expands out of this simple picture. Everything is designed to enable us to see better, ask why better, or put our understanding into form better. This is the simplicity at the heart of lean development.

To understand better why conventional organizations don't perform the value-adding cycle very well, let's expand it a little.

Expressed this way, the cycle includes:

- Observing product physics, competitive products, customer behavior, manufacturing processes, suppliers, nature, new technology.
- Inventing something to take advantage of the new knowledge —a new geometry, parts organization, theory.
- Testing the invention, in analysis, hardware, simulation.
- Abstracting the knowledge acquired into compact, easily understood, usable form.
- Connecting what we've learned to existing theory.
- Teaching what we've learned to others.
- Observing again.

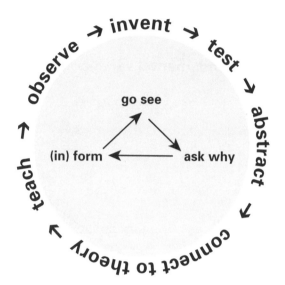

To be really effective, you have to complete the whole cycle. Most conventional managers and engineers aren't even aware of some important pieces.

The problem begins in the first grade, where innocent children are taught that learning means regurgitating what the teacher said. It intensifies in engineering. The Merriam-Webster definition of engineering is "the practical application of scientific and mathematical principles."

This assumes that the scientific and mathematical principles are already known. But the known principles provide little competitive advantage, because the competition knows them too! Competitive advantage derives from discovering new principles, specific to your products and obtainable only from your experience. Of course, these new principles build on and require general "book" knowledge—they connect to theory—but engineers have to *learn* them the same way Newton and Maxwell learned. Discovering how to stamp steel well uses the same mental process as discovering Newton's laws.

Such learning produces the deep, detailed knowledge of lean companies. Denso, Toyota's largest supplier, runs an internal university, offering advanced education in mechanical and electrical engineering. When I asked whether Denso used professors from nearby Nagoya University to teach the courses, Denso engineers said, "No. We tried that, but the professors don't know enough. All our courses are taught by our managers." Then they smiled apologetically, because I was a professor at the time![9]

Unfortunately, few engineering students learn how to learn unless they go on to get a doctorate (and often not then). The best engineers can do most of the cycle. They learned how to invent before they ever went to school, and academia couldn't beat it out of them. They learn to observe, test, and connect theory to observation once they go to work. But very few ever learn to abstract or to teach—to turn data into usable knowledge.

Business schools often are even worse. The case study method trains future managers to analyze a written story, make a decision, and defend it. But, since the story has already been written, someone has already done the *observing* and much of the *abstracting*. Worse, class grades are based on the persuasiveness of the argument; there is no way to actually test the proposed solution.

In real developments, the market and Mother Nature test the solution vigorously. Most markets yield surprisingly little to persuasion. Many companies have come to grief by assuming that strong advertising could compensate for weak products. Mother Nature doesn't pay attention to persuasion at all. Skill in "making the case" helps MBAs compete inside conventional companies, but often it hurts the company in competing with others because a good argument often defeats good judgment.

I'm not attacking formal education, just noting its limits. (You may be encouraged to know that Japanese education is probably worse at teaching the learning cycle than American education—though generally better at teaching facts.) Lean companies know that they, not the educational system, have to teach developers how to learn. *This is the primary source of lean competitive advantage.*

---

9. Reference here, the editors believe, is to Denso's in-house training, which traditionally is taught by internal managers.

DO

Create the core vision

Publicize both versions of the basic value-adding cycle. Explain to people: "This is what we are trying to do. Every part of lean development is there to make us better at this—and if we are getting better at this, we are getting leaner, regardless of whether we are learning any Japanese words or not." This is the core of your vision of the future.

Teach your people how to do trade-off curves (coming soon, when we talk about set-based concurrent engineering). Grade your organization on both versions of the valuing-creating cycle, and work at the weak points:

- If your organization doesn't "go see" well, get out of your office and go see yourself, dragging people with you.

- If it is weak at invention, make a point of dropping by desks and asking people what ideas they have produced.

- It if is weak at abstracting and teaching what it has learned, ask that your subordinates teach you and everyone else who could benefit.

- Above all, look carefully at trade-off curve sheets whenever you can, and ask "why" at least once every three minutes.

That is the simple version of how to learn. Now, what are you supposed to learn about?

Lean design is system design

Where should you focus your learning efforts?

Everyone knows that Toyota is very good at details. That's ironic because what Toyota really is good at is system design. The details always are pulled by the connections.

Definition: System design deals with the way things fit and work together.

A good system designer will rarely choose the supplier with the lowest price, even if cost is important to the product. Price is an isolated property of the part: It has little effect on how the part works in the system as a whole. Suppose a part involves 10% of the cost of the product—increasing the part cost by 10% will increase the product cost by only 1%. The effect is isolated.

Conversely, if the part fails in service, the whole product fails. If the supplier delivers the part late, the whole product is late. If the part design doesn't fit well into the system design, the customer is likely to be dissatisfied with the whole system. Quality, timing, and design integration are strongly interactive properties, not isolated ones. A good system designer will pay more attention to quality, delivery, and the supplier's ability to work creatively on the design team—the way things work together more than to isolated part properties such as price. Interactive properties have more effect on profit than isolated ones.

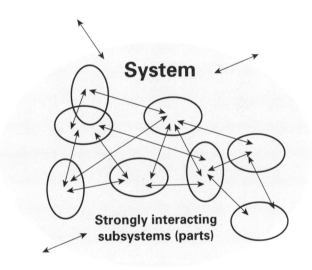

System designers may put a boundary around any convenient group of physical or conceptual objects and interactions and call them a system. A system can be any size, from a proton to a single human cell to a nation to the universe. Every system is part of an environment or supersystem; every system has parts or subsystems. Strong interactions among objects make it useful to see them as a system, but almost all systems have some interactions that extend through their boundaries. Systems often overlap. For instance, wheels are part of the drive train system but also part of the suspension system.

We will move freely between different size systems. I'll write *the system* to mean whatever we are talking about designing at the moment, whether it is a screw, a manufacturing process or machine, a fuel system, an engine, a complete drive train, a car, airplane, or complete transportation system, or the complete operational value stream for any of these. I hope this won't confuse readers who are accustomed to using *system* only for cars, airplanes, or computers. Here, a car will be a *subsystem* if we are talking about designing its complete value stream, and a *supersystem* if we are talking about designing a power train.

The rest of this section discusses three aspects of system—value stream—design:

- Aligning a coherent operational value stream.

- Aligning the company behind projects and project leaders—without destroying its ability to learn.

- Integrating suppliers to enhance their learning ability.

The value stream must "line-up"

What do development projects create? A complete value stream "... *specific* products with *specific* capabilities offered at *specific* prices through a dialog with *specific* customers," (Womack and Jones, *Lean Thinking*), made in *specific* plants using *specific* operations and machines with *specific* capabilities on parts and materials bought from *specific* suppliers with their own *specific* capabilities. (Got the point? I promise to use the word "specific" only once more.)

Value streams succeed if all of those specific characteristics are aligned. (That was it.) Projects and practices fail when they optimize one part of the value stream at the expense of others or when the parts just don't fit—luxury customers with low-cost and low-quality suppliers, for example.

"Alignment maps" can help line up all of the pieces of the value stream. Let's look at the features of the following example.

In this alignment map, each row represents a different potential customer (save for the last row, which is a summary conclusion). We start with customer needs and competitor analysis, then work our way left, first to our product features/limits, then to key features/limits of our production facility, and finally to important supplier features/limits. Company names are italicized. The column labels A-I are provided for ease of reference.

A	B Supplier Features (limits)	C	D Plant Features (limits)	E	F Product Features (limits)	G	H Customer Needs (limits)	I Competitors' Weaknesses (strengths)
I	*AnD:* Precision analog-to-digital converters *Hardshell:* Noise shielding cases (high cost)	I	Plant A: Laser trimming (vol=300/day)	I	Flexibility through modularity	*If not Cost*	HI-Flex: Flexibility (10/day)	
				I	Precision through laser-trimmed components	I	*Acme:* High-precision; moderate flexibility; 100/day	
				O	Low cost	O	*Syndyne:* Precision; 1200/day	*Rex & Ruins:* Inflexible (*Syndyne* likes them) (Cost 20% below ours)
			Volume needed: 200/day				Volume targeted: 100/day	

Column H describes the particular needs of each customer, together with factors (in parenthesis) that may cause problems.

Column G shows whether we are going after this customer: I (in), O (out), or C for contracted. Blank means we haven't decided yet. We have special note for Hi-Flex: We will pursue their low volume only if we can do so without adding significant cost. (Why not just erase customers we won't pursue? Because we need a record of the decision, and we may change our minds.)

Column I reflects competitors, and shows why we gave up on Syndyne. Syndyne already is buying from Rex & Ruins, a ferocious competitor much better fitted than we to Syndyne's relatively high-volume needs.

Columns E and F show that we have decided to compete on the basis of flexibility and precision. We do not expect to be the low-cost competitor. (This doesn't mean we don't care about cost. But we have to choose where we intend to win. Design involves trade-offs.)

Columns C and D show that we've chosen plant A, which provides the needed laser trimming to achieve the high precision.

Columns A and B show that we have chosen AnD as supplier of the high-precision analog-to-digital converters we need. We haven't yet ruled Hardshell in or out.

Row 5 shows that we are in trouble. We need to produce 200/day; we have customers only for 100/day. We can either find more customers or we can get a lot smaller, fast.

Use alignment maps to align projects and product lines with reality

Do an alignment map for every project and product line. Use the alignment map to guide lean projects from project start. Use it to kill bad conventional projects. Most conventional companies have many projects that will not repay more investment. These compete for resources with potentially profitable lean projects. Get rid of them. Stop chasing business that you can't compete successfully in, or business that no one else wants because the volumes are too low or the customer too distant and unreliable.

If that leaves you with no way to meet your volume needs, it is time for some hard decisions. You may have to get smaller. You may have to take some losses while you conduct "strategic development," discussed when we get to set-based concurrent engineering. You may have to hire some knowledge away from competitors or consultants.

Don't try to get out of the problem by being everything to everyone. That just makes it worse. So, usually, does radically changing business direction, or firing all of your most experienced people. You may not be very good at using your knowledge because you don't know how to abstract it. But you actually have a lot of knowledge buried in your people's heads. This book will teach you how to make that knowledge useable—so don't throw it away.

Many companies make the most elementary alignment mistakes usually because of poor communications within the company. Marketing sees a great opportunity in a desperate customer, not noticing that their volume or feature needs are a terrible fit to our capabilities. Purchasing sees a low-cost supplier—and doesn't notice that the supplier cannot enhance our reputation with the customer. Engineering tries to build in features we don't understand well—and a competitor does.

Of course, this is a hard and risky business. Alignment is rarely perfect. But unless you constantly work toward alignment, you'll drift away from it. This produces loss of profit and market share, followed by a desperate effort to find someone to buy the product, further reducing the alignment, driving more desperate sales efforts, and so on—another version of the death spiral. "Relax and level the wings"—in other words, stop doing those things that make the situation worse and take measured corrective action; which is, in this case, value-stream alignment.

Now for a different kind of alignment—the alignment of the company behind projects and project leaders.

Aligning the business behind projects

How are lean companies organized, and how do they reconcile specialized expertise and value stream-system-focus?

Development project teams deliver knowledge-value to the operations department, just as manufacturing cells deliver value to final customers. Everything in the company needs to support development teams and manufacturing cells—they are where the value is added.

The project leader is the key to aligning the business. In lean companies, project leaders are both entrepreneurs responsible for project profit and system designers responsible for designing the value stream. At Toyota they call their project leaders "chief engineers," and they say, "It's the chief engineer's car." Later, we'll discuss at length what project leaders do.

But lean companies also need strong functional departments (for example, body engineering, styling, or manufacturing engineering) to build knowledge. Pure product line organizations have great difficulty learning across projects. Chrysler saw great initial success with its platform team organization but couldn't sustain it. So, most lean developers work in functional departments for functional managers (or for suppliers) —a conventional-looking chain of command. Chief engineers supervise only a few assistants.

Each of the Toyota vehicle design centers (front-wheel drive, rear-wheel drive, and truck) looks something like this:[10]

10. Since the writing of the original manuscript, Toyota has restructured its product development organization. However, the basic design philosophy of strong functional groups that house most of the developers, with crosscutting project leaders for major vehicle programs, still holds.

Departments Chief engineers	Body	Interior	Styling	Powertrain	Chassis
Corolla					
Camry					

"Aha," you say. "A matrix. We tried that, and it didn't work. (I knew this guy Ward wasn't so smart.)"

But it isn't a matrix, despite appearances! Everyone has only one boss. The departments, not the chief engineers, rate the people on the teams. And, the chief engineers' technical influence extends far beyond the development center. For example, manufacturing engineers work outside the development centers—in different cities, for different vice presidents. Yet, chief engineers work the same way with product engineers and manufacturing engineers. The chief engineer designs the system, integrating the parts of the system. Period.

Why not use a matrix structure?

- Matrix organizations don't work. Trying to work for two different bosses drives people crazy. They spend even more time on nonvalue-adding efforts to please the bosses.

- The value-stream leaders should be too busy designing the value stream to manage the developers.

- Developers naturally tend to focus their effort on "finishing" the current project, making the decisions, finishing the drawings. They need functional managers to hold their attention on creating the knowledge that will prevent future problems.

- Specialists need to be able to tell the value-stream designers that they are wrong, and force compromise.

But, without a matrix structure—without formal power over the developers—how do the value-stream leaders get the support they need?

Through the "cycle of support."

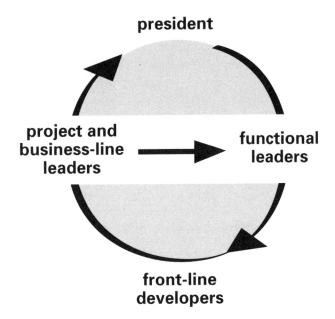

The president of the company is responsible for making money and for all the value streams. He supports the functional leaders, supplying resources and an overall vision of the company's future.

Value-stream designers—**project and business-line leaders** like Toyota's chief engineers—support the president, usually through a vice president for development. Like the president, they are responsible for making money.

Front-line developers—working engineers, purchasing agents, marketing researchers —support the value-stream designers. They create most of the knowledge value that goes into the product.

Functional—departmental—leaders support the frontline developers by helping them to organize their knowledge across projects and funding concept work not yet ready for projects, thus building capability to better support future projects. They negotiate with the value-stream designers to provide appropriate resources. And they keep the value-stream leaders from making serious mistakes.

Conventional bureaucratic thinking tends to focus on *"what does my boss want?"* Lean thinking tends to focus on *"what do my customers—the people I support with my knowledge—need?"* I had dinner once with a pair of Toyota general managers of styling and body engineering.

They had obviously worked together a lot, happily, and successfully. When I asked where their chains of command intersected in a common boss, they didn't know. Toyota manages tight cooperation between widely separated parts of the organization.

Customers are different from bosses, partly because the customer isn't always right. Functional leaders and value-stream designers frequently come into conflict. The project and product line leaders are responsible for and have the most knowledge of the value stream as a whole. But the functional leaders have the responsibility and specific expertise to make the parts of the value stream work—and all of the parts have to work, or the value stream doesn't work. So there is no rule for deciding who is right—they have to work it out, finding a solution that works from every perspective.

Functional leaders have to support value-stream leaders because the support cycle is a closed loop. The president is in frequent communication with the value-stream leaders, and gets feedback on how well the functional leaders are doing their jobs. (Evaluating the value stream leaders is easy. Either their value streams make money, or they don't.) So the question "what does my boss want?" has a standard answer: My boss wants me to serve my customers well—including by telling them when they are wrong.

Align the organization around projects and product lines

This is a big one and will take a while to fully implement. The key is the relationship among the president, the value-stream leaders, and the department leaders.

Publicize the support cycle concept. Get a discussion going.

Train project and business line leaders, using the entrepreneur system-designer concepts, which we'll discuss later.

Try to get agreement, from the top down, to the following:

Responsibilities
- *Value-stream leaders* will take responsibility for profit, for satisfying customers, and the overall system design of the value stream. The president will hold them responsible.

- *Departmental (functional) leaders* will take responsibility for supporting value-stream leaders with current and future knowledge. This includes developing concepts and trade-off curves continuously, preventing value-stream leaders from making mistakes, and negotiating win-win compromises. The president will hold them responsible.

- *Every development project* will be assigned a team with required expertise; from beginning to end, without worrying about which department the expertise comes from. Adding value will take precedence over departmental boundaries.

- *Each developer* will be on few enough teams that they can support them effectively.

- *Project and business-line leaders* will negotiate resources and goals directly with appropriate functional leaders.

Beliefs and behaviors

- Re-organizations, plans and programs, procedures, and corporate politics are at best a lower priority, if not just waste. No one will be promoted without clear evidence of significant contribution to a value stream.

- "Bosses" support their people in supporting their knowledge customers; the boss is happy if the customers are happy.

You can count on backsliding, so enforce the agreement by surfacing and negotiating problems.

Designing manufacturing systems

Focusing on the complete value stream elevates the role of manufacturing system design.

Customers don't normally buy designs; they buy products that are manufactured by manufacturing systems. Capital cost is normally a dominant factor in profitability. The Ford world car (Contour, Mondeo, Mystique), for example, was a $6 billion development project, a sum that never will be recouped.

Toyota's manufacturing systems consistently produce the highest quality in the world, yet their capital expenditures are far below U.S. norms.

How does Toyota do it, and how can you?

1. Innovation in manufacturing is as important as innovation in products. Manufacturing innovations contribute tremendously to reduced costs and allow product innovations. They are easier than product innovations to keep secret and can therefore supply more prolonged competitive advantage. Assign manufacturing engineers to projects from the beginning. If possible, separate manufacturing engineers into *plant support engineers*, who work for the plant manager; and *central manufacturing* engineering, which supports projects. Rotate people back and forth.

2. When designing products, developers are designing for an existing manufacturing process and must be guided by the knowledge of the manufacturing engineers. Demand trade-off curve sheets to tell the product developers what they can and can't do.

3. Close the loop between designing things and making things. Sometimes, prototype parts should be made in production facilities; often they should be made on prototype or partially complete production equipment. Plant operators, team leaders, and maintenance people are the ultimate authorities on how equipment actually is used and maintained. Assign them to every major development team from the beginning. Use them to advise on manufacturability, development procedures, and training plans, and to make prototype parts.

4. Try to design and build any tooling that is intimately connected with parts or assemblies you build. For example, Toyota and Honda both design and build stamping dies, robotic welding systems, and engine transfer lines—but, they don't design stamping equipment. This close connection between manufacturing, product design, and tooling design enables much more rapid learning. Some estimates say Toyota and Honda tooling equipment is as much as 70% lighter and cheaper than conventional. At worst, form an extremely tight relationship with one or two suppliers, buying a piece of them if you have to, and bring them deeply into your system.

5. Design manufacturing systems to fight the production wastes mentioned earlier. Read *Learning to See* (Shook and Rother) and *Creating Continuous Flow* (Rother and Harris) both available from The Lean Enterprise Institute, but here's a very brief introduction:

   • Against the wastes of overproduction, inventory, space, and motion, try to use U-shaped cells rather than conveyor lines or fully automated equipment. The operators in a U-shaped cell move minimum distances inside the U, manually loading the relatively simple equipment. It is easy to change the number of operators to adjust to changes in demand if need be; a single person can operate the entire cell. If possible, design for *single-piece flow*, so that an operator picking up a part from one machine immediately loads it into the next.

- Also against overproduction and inventory, design for rapid changeover if the equipment must produce multiple parts. (A simple system dedicated to a single product is better, but often impossible. Die stamping, for example, is so much faster than assembly that die exchange is required.)

- Against the wastes of defects and waiting, concentrate on the reliability of equipment. Run at lower speeds. Add simple devices to ensure that parts are properly loaded and to stop machines if anything goes wrong. Automatically unload machines. Have operators move from machine to machine, constantly adding value, rather than watching a single machine work.

- Design for the low end of possible volumes and lifespans. If the product turns out to be more popular than expected, you can always build another copy of the production system and still make money. But an expensive, automated system designed for high volume will lose big at low volume.

6. Integrate the construction and testing of the equipment into the development process if possible. If you can get a simple, low-cost system up and running early in development, you will be able to add error-proofing devices and make modifications to improve its performance during the development. If you wait until close to the start of production, you have to over-design the equipment, trying to anticipate everything that could go wrong—and mostly likely missing something.

Build your machines from standardized, easily combined and separated parts so that you can easily change them as the project evolves. Build first the parts of the system that are most certain; plan to quickly construct those that can't be frozen until late in the process. Also, consider building machines in the order of production operations, so that you can use them to construct prototypes.

7. Have everyone get their hands dirty. Break down the barriers and distinctions between managers, engineers, technicians, and operators. Give everyone frequent experience in actually using products. There is simply no substitute for learning directly from experience—nor for understanding the underlying theory. We need both. Edison, the Wright brothers, Henry Ford, and Bill Gates lacked higher education but accomplished far more than their better educated counterparts because they were able to integrate theory with hands-on action.

Build a lean community in your company

Form an alliance with the lean manufacturing enthusiasts in your company and outside it.

If you aren't already educating your engineers about lean manufacturing, start. Until product and manufacturing system design are fully integrated out of habit, hold periodic workshops and design reviews to ensure integration.

As always, be cautious in re-organizing but move toward the organizational concepts discussed above. Use the personnel rotation concepts we'll talk about under "pull, flow, and cadence" to achieve the benefits of re-organization without actually re-organizing. Get the whole value-stream involved and communicating.

"Design-in" suppliers add knowledge-value

Most industrial companies pay more for purchased parts than for labor, capital equipment, or anything else—so their greatest opportunities to increase profit lie in decreasing part cost. But conventional cost-reduction efforts frequently backfire; quality drops, or suppliers go bankrupt, cut funds for research and independent development, or look for other customers. Toyota, conversely, has maintained long and mutually profitable relationships with its suppliers. How?

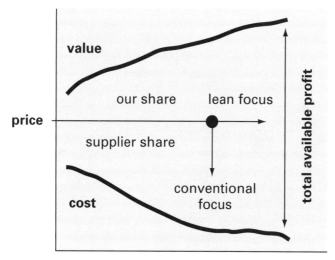

Definition: *total available profit* is the difference between the part value and the part cost. The price of the parts splits the total available profit between buying company and supplier. Conventional purchasing focuses primarily on reducing the price—increasing the purchaser's share at the expense of the supplier. Lean companies pay attention to the price, but focus more strongly on increasing the knowledge of both companies, thus increasing the total available profit.

Supplier and purchasing company must learn to:

- Integrate the component into the system (that is, our product).

- Design the part to achieve the desired functionality for the final customer.

- Design the product and manufacturing system combination for minimum cost and maximum quality.

- Negotiate a mutually profitable price.

Let's look at these issues through a series of decisions.

	Make Ourselves	Supplier Make
Design Ourselves	1) Tightly integrated, tricky manufacturing, expertise and capacity possible; or 2) Critical, expertise possible, can't safely buy the expertise; or 3) An appropriate supplier doesn't exist	1) Design and build similar parts or, 2) System integrating harder than design for functionality and manufacture (machine bases)
Supplier Design	Supplier has special design competence, we have capacity (furniture companies); should develop more expertise.	Default 1) Integration easier than design for functionality and manufacture (computer parts); or 2) Too hard for us

First, we must decide whether to buy the component and its design at all. We should both *design* and *make* the component in three cases (*top left in the table*).

1) The component is high value, "tightly integrated" into the system, and design for manufacture is relatively tricky. In this case, we probably must become experts. For example, auto bodies touch and influence every system in the car, and their cost is highly dependent on subtle issues of design. A car company that doesn't make its own bodies loses too many opportunities to learn about integration and manufacturing and quickly will fall behind. Lean companies also normally design and build their own tooling; in this case, Toyota and Honda design their own stamping dies.

2) The component is a large fraction of the product value or functionality, we are able and willing to learn to be experts at it, and depending on a supplier's expertise, might be extremely expensive. For example, Toyota builds engines because they are experts, and it is profitable. Toyota apparently chose to build the electronic controller for the Prius hybrid-electric car because they had no expertise and were afraid to be dependent on so critical a component without understanding it.

3) We can't find an appropriate supplier.

At lower left, office furniture companies often make a product but *farm out the design*. They need to be large in order to make the product but believe they are not as creative as a small company. Moving to lean development should reduce the creativity differential; however, lean companies should generally move away from this quadrant.

At top right belong cases where we *design* and *make* similar parts and simply need more capacity. Toyota outsources some body construction but is prepared to teach the supplier how to "do it right." Sometimes, system integration is relatively complex compared with part functionality and design for manufacture, so we should design the parts because we have more of the relevant knowledge.

Often, this is because the supplier has provided semi-standard designs, with instructions for customizing them—for example, with machine bases. Suppliers have a set of semi-standard designs, so the customer need only know enough to choose a frame size and type and specify a surface flatness and a mounting hole pattern. Mounting holes are a system-integration issue involving a lot of detail that the customer wants to keep changing until the last minute, but the design for manufacture and functionality issues have been taken care of in the supplier's standard design instructions.

The bottom right quadrant is the default we should buy both *design* and *make* whenever we can. Why? Because it reduces the amount that we have to learn.

We may have the supplier design and manufacture because:

- Integration into the system is easier than design for manufacture or functionality. For example, personal computer makers don't design or manufacture any parts except possibly cases because the interfaces are so well standardized that integration is relatively easy.

- We just can't afford to develop the expertise, or the capacity. In the extreme case, we may have to design the system around the component; personal computers are designed around microprocessors.

Once we've decided the supplier should *design* and *make* the part, we have a second choice. When will the parts be designed, relative to the system design?

There are three choices:

- Specified parts are designed after the system;
- Cataloged parts are designed before the system;
- Design-in parts are designed together with the system.

Design-in actually begins before system design. Design-in suppliers hold a design show each year for Toyota, showcasing their new technologies. And it extends after the system design essentially is complete, as suppliers tweak their designs to optimize the system. But the heart of design-in is a prolonged process of considering different alternatives for both the system and the parts, eliminating concepts that don't work well together.

Thus, design-in involves adjusting the subsystem design to meet the needs of the system, and the system design to meet the needs of the subsystem. It offers a much better chance to learn how to integrate the system and part—which offers the most leverage for increasing total available profit. If their volumes are large enough to justify a special design, lean companies use design-in for most major subsystems.

So when should you use each type of part?

Specified parts: Rarely. Specifying parts reduces your ability to learn from the supplier how to make best use of the part in your system. It reduces the time available for the supplier to learn. And it opens you to tremendous risk. What if you have predicated your system design on specifications that it turns out the supplier can't meet?

Of course, you can safely "specify" really trivial parts, where you know the design can meet the spec—but this is usually more like buying from a catalog.

Cataloged parts: Whenever they can be made to fit the system without too much performance or cost penalty. Using cataloged parts enables you to draw on the learning curve of others; the supplier doesn't need to learn how to design for performance and manufacturing at your expense. It also reduces risk.

Design-in parts: When there is enough to be gained from adjusting the system and the parts to each other to justify the cost—and you can find an appropriate supplier to work with.

Lean development thus turns conventional system design on its head. Rather than designing the system, and then specifying components to fit in to it, we either fit the system to available components, or design them both together. We'll talk later about the technical details of how to make this work (set-based concurrent engineering). For now, let's ask about its consequences for supplier relationships.

We are at the third decision. Should you aim at:

1) Buying from the supplier offering the lowest price; or

2) Establishing an intimate learning relationship with one to two-and-a-half suppliers, while paying a fair price?

Definition: A fair price is close to long-run market price, and gives you and your suppliers the same overall profitability—if you both do a good job.

(Extraordinary performance merits a higher fraction of the total available profit, and weak performance merits a lower fraction. But you have to be honest and objective in evaluating performance.)

Lean companies almost always choose alternative 2. Why?

First, let's look at the problems with conventional practice—alternative 1.

- You and the supplier have a powerful incentive to hide information from each other because knowledge is power in negotiations. This makes learning very hard.

- You wind up working with many different suppliers, so it is really hard for you or them to learn much.

- It's impossible to design-in. With design-in, you don't know what you want to buy, so suppliers can't compete to offer it at the lowest possible price.

- If the parts are specified, you can go out for bid. However, you are relying on the supplier's promise to deliver. Since bids are distributed around the "sensible" bid, the winners generally made a mistake and underbid. They normally will find a way to cheat on the promise. (Consider that buildings constructed to sealed bid are notoriously undependable.) If they can't cheat, they are likely to go bankrupt, and you have to learn to work with another supplier.

- If the parts are from catalogs, you can buy the cheapest and get what you pay for. But since cataloged parts usually are sold to many customers that collectively have many alternatives, they already have been subject to heavy price pressure, and the cheapest may well be genuinely inferior. Further, chasing the cheapest means that you have to learn about multiple supplier products.

In contrast, following fair-pricing policies with a few suppliers makes it much easier to learn and is essential to design-in. How do you get a fair price?

- *Pick suppliers on performance, not promises.* Their willingness to share information, the technology they have developed, the quality and responsiveness they have delivered, the prices they have charged in the past, and their own lean initiatives are your best indicators of what you can expect.

- *Make sure design-in suppliers are geographically close.* Flying to Mexico every time you need to learn something can quickly eat up the difference in labor rates, which are temporary anyway. Geographic proximity also reduces inventory and defects.

- *Go with a single supplier only for cataloged parts*, where the market as a whole can provide discipline, or the supplier is unusually good, and you can get other sources of leverage, such as partial ownership and a dominant position as a customer (i.e., buying 60% of the supplier's output). Otherwise, maintain two suppliers for each kind of part (though only one should work with a given project), and be constantly looking around to see if you should replace one of them with an outsider.

- *Know how much it should cost to make your parts.* Learn what similar parts cost. Demand that your suppliers explain their costs in detail. This will allow you to adjust the system design to minimize their costs, and will help you to know whether you are being overcharged. Again, you need to shoot for a fair price rather than the lowest possible price; otherwise, the supplier will be forced to hide information from you.

- *Create a target price tree for the whole system*: The product will sell for X; fair profit requires that all the subsystems be bought for Y; supplier A's fair share of that is Z. Raise prices from the target only if the supplier delivers a lot more value than expected or faces unexpected costs that aren't the suppliers' fault (in this case, you may want to share the loss with the supplier—if the long-term relationship justifies it).

- *Focus purchasing representatives on the "company-to-company" relationship*; let engineers handle most of the part-by-part communication. The engineers need to work out the system integration, and the target price tree will prevent them from serious mistakes. Purchasing needs to focus on making sure that you are buying at a profitable price overall from each supplier; suppliers that do better on average should get more business.

- *Learn from your suppliers, and help your suppliers to learn*, especially about how to integrate their parts into your systems. Make sure they get their share of any information flowing from field experience; take them along on tests. If you have special strengths in lean manufacturing, you can help them out. They will have to learn about lean development in order to do design-in effectively.

Implement lean supplier relationships

You need design-in relationships now. Encourage commodity buyers and project leaders to work together to find suppliers that you can safely bring on board at the beginning of the project, with only a target price and a general concept to guide them. Explain your vision to your suppliers, watch them closely to see how open and reliable they are, and be open and reliable with them.

Maintain a central knowledge base of experience with each supplier. Review it periodically. You probably won't have much trouble narrowing the field.

Value focus pulls the system

This section looked at value focus—focus creating usable knowledge about the wh
value stream. This is the central principle of lean development because it *pulls* the v
rest of the system:

- The entrepreneur system designers cut across departmental boundaries to create integration knowledge and enforce the value focus on the entire stream.

- Set-based concurrent engineering provides rapid learning and robustness through redundant concepts at every level of the system, coupled with aggressive elimination of weak concepts.

- Cadence, pull, and flow eliminate wasteful management structures and reports. Because they are cyclic, they allow continuous improvement, steadily reducing waste.

- The team of responsible experts creates and teaches knowledge that contributes to robust profitability. The personnel management system rewards this. The functional, departmental managers of the organization act primarily to lead that knowledge-creating process.

Let's turn next to the people primarily responsible for the success of future value streams: the value-stream designers, or entrepreneur system designers.

Entrepreneur system designers

Your company probably has people responsible for learning about customers, for product engineering and manufacturing engineering knowledge, and for learning about suppliers—though they might not see learning as their primary function. But what is the most important knowledge about? In your company, who is responsible for learning how to fit all the parts of the value stream together?

Usually, no one—so conventional companies optimize parts of the system at the expense of the whole. For example, a senior executive at Toyota told me that he had torn down a 1996 Taurus—the model year that converted American's most popular car into a money loser. "Each part of the car," he said, "is world class. It looks as if functional leaders responsible for the parts demanded excellence, knowing that the car was very important to Ford. Yet, when you put all the excellent parts together, the result isn't a very good car. The project must have had a weak chief engineer."

He did not know that at the time, Ford's chief engineers primarily were bureaucrats; they are not responsible for the system design. System design at Ford was divided among Marketing, which was primarily responsible for the specifications; Styling, which determined the shape; and Advanced Engineering, which defined the basic arrangement of the mechanical systems and the room available for each. So, there was no one who could really define a vision for the car, and make appropriate trade-offs between, say, Styling's desire for an appealing shape and Marketing's desire for good handling—let alone Manufacturing's desire for an easily assembled suspension system and Purchasing's desire for low-cost parts.

The same logic applies even to the smallest components. Any component and its value stream are a system and need a system designer.

Now, ask yourself another question. *"Who in my company is responsible for making money from each project?"* The usual answer is "everyone"—which means no one. And how could there be, if there is no one responsible for designing the entire value stream?

In contrast, consider startup companies such as my machine design and build company. The president is the project leader, and absolutely is responsible for profit and satisfying customers. Successful presidents are almost always system designers. (Both MIT and the Harvard Business School are located in the same hot-bed of entrepreneurship—yet almost all of the companies along the famous Massachusetts "Technology Highway" were founded by MIT engineers.)

Why are successful company founders good system designers? Because customers pay for the system, not the parts.

A good project leader—or start-up company president—must:

Create and communicate a new, compelling, and feasible vision of a profitable value stream, customers, product features, manufacturing processes, and suppliers. (In the '90s, dozens of would be start-up leaders forgot the "feasible" requirement for a good vision.)

Inspire excellent developers, who have a burning desire to create great products, with the burning desire to create the leader's product. Leaders must be so in love with the future product that they inspire this love or at least faith in others—which is why they are also usually the firm's best sales representatives.

- *Define a clear and logical "architecture" for the product and value stream.* Why will it satisfy customers? What customers? What will the pieces be, and how will they fit together? What underlying technical philosophy will make the system coherent? What are the targets for the system and each of its parts?

- *Quickly learn just enough about many technologies and functions to solve cross-disciplinary problems.* This requires deep technical and business insight—the ability to see that a new situation is governed by familiar physical and human principles.

- *Control the development process,* keeping the process moving, avoiding waste.

- *Make fast and correct decisions,* balancing innovation, risk, time, cost, customer needs, and product and manufacturing physics.

- *Provide technical guidance to the different departments,* translate between them, and forge their conflicts into compromise or consensus.

These are exactly the skills of a good system designer, combined with those of an entrepreneur! Of course, the skills that control risk, satisfy customers, and make money.

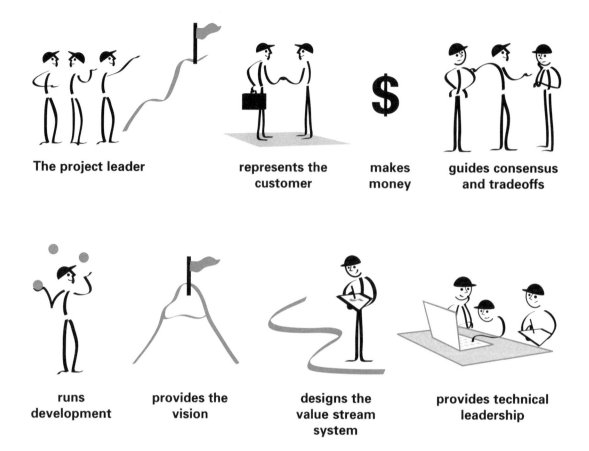

The project leader   **represents the customer**   **makes money**   **guides consensus and tradeoffs**

runs development   **provides the vision**   **designs the value stream system**   **provides technical leadership**

So, lean companies choose system designers as project leaders and make them responsible for making money from the project. Honda calls them "large scale project leaders."[11] Toyota calls them "chief engineers," and says, *"It's the chief engineer's car."* The chief engineer is responsible for profitability, system architecture, (he signs every drawing), project planning and timing, negotiating for resources with the departmental leaders, achieving consensus in the design team, and even approving the initial marketing campaign.

In contrast, large conventional companies often make an irrecoverable mistake: They aim project leaders at satisfying management rather than customers; at administering the project rather than designing the system. Conventional project leaders fill out the forms, chase the work and the missing parts, nag the engineers to meet the specifications, track the deliverables, and answer management's questions. They typically are responsible for meeting cost and performance specifications set by someone else. (These mean they can't be held responsible for making money

11. This was the author's understanding at the time of writing.

because the right targets are part of an entrepreneur system designer's vision.) They often are bored, and they bore the development team, reducing progress to a crawl. (In development, there is no substitute for excitement.)

Therefore, you must select, train, and manage project leaders as *entrepreneur system designers*. They have to design the value stream, and they have to take responsibility for profit.

If you have too many projects for a vice president for development to supervise and support, you also will need business line leaders to take responsibility for clusters of projects. These also are entrepreneur system designers; good bureaucrats often are disastrous as business-line leaders. The exact division of responsibility between project leaders and business-line leaders may vary between companies. For example, at one time Toyota refreshed cars on a four-year cycle but needed much less time to do a project. Toyota therefore started using chief engineers to supervise a small cluster of product lines, blurring the distinction between project and business-line leader.[12]

One major problem is that business-line leaders may be responsible for present value streams as well as future ones; and even project leaders may have current responsibilities, for example for delivering prototypes to customers. Present urgency often overcomes future importance, and creating knowledge takes a back seat to meeting deliverables and fighting fires.

To protect the future from the present, plant managers can sometimes take on management of current value streams. Production control and logistics or the leadership of the prototype shop or an assistant project leader may take responsibility for providing customers with prototypes. Business-line managers can have assistants to deal with either current or future issues. Or, they can set aside half of each day to focus on the future and be very careful to shield project leaders from present issues. Whatever the organizational structure, the entrepreneur system designers need to focus the bulk of their time and effort on creating new system knowledge for effective future value streams.

We've already discussed, back in Part 1, how the organization needs to support project leaders. Without support, they will fail. Now, let's look at little deeper at the psychology involved.

---

12. Since the writing of the original manuscript, Toyota has restructured its product development organization. However, the basic design philosophy of strong functional groups that house most of the developers, with crosscutting project leaders for major vehicle programs, still holds.

The psychology of organizational tension

Why aren't entrepreneur system designers (ESDs) already running your projects and business lines? After all, ESDs start most companies, and they probably are responsible whenever a mature company does something really good. Yet, mature conventional companies don't systematically develop, select, and support them.

For example: Kelly Johnson, chief engineer and head of the skunkworks at Lockheed, was a great ESD. He created many of the world's finest airplanes, including the SR-71 Blackbird, still the fastest airplane on earth four decades later. Yet, Lockheed replaced him with a business leader—a nice guy and a capable manager—who had few of his system design skills. In 1995, Lockheed merged with Martin Marietta to form Lockheed Martin.

Ford was founded by a great ESD, Henry Ford. More recently, Lew Veraldi, ESD for the original 1984 Ford Taurus, changed the way automobiles look, created the world's best-selling car, and perhaps saved Ford from bankruptcy. Yet he retired immediately after the project, and the Taurus began losing money. Why didn't Ford systematize his role, using entrepreneur system designers as project leaders for every project?

Ford (and GM) have tried to establish ESDs. In the 1990s Ford appointed "vehicle line directors" (GM, "vehicle line executives") to take entrepreneurial responsibility for each project. But, they separated these roles from the role of chief engineer—system designer. They hoped that the two would work effectively together to perform the ESD function. It hasn't worked very well.[13]

13. The financial woes of Ford and General Motors in 2006, at the time of printing, reflect how acutely accurate the author's insights were five years earlier. While much of the business press seems to have focused on "business issues" such as outsourcing, supply base, and bloated pension plans, the fact remains that neither company has created consistently profitable value streams.

The GM executive in charge of the Vehicle Line Executive program told me he split the business and system design roles. GM does not have leaders who combined the required business and technical skills. But business objectives in manufacturing companies can be accomplished only through system-design skills. It is precisely the ability to formulate a compelling but realistic vision and make good trade-offs that enables profitable products. "Product visions" are just hot air unless they are inspired by engineering imagination and infused with engineering judgment. And products are engineers' toys unless they are informed by business vision and business judgment. The combination makes the successful system. The project leader must be both entrepreneur and a system designer.

It is very rare for two people to be so close that they can "think as one" well enough to effectively implement this combination—much rarer than individuals who have both skill sets.

GM is a big company. I believe there were plenty of potential ESDs. But if not, why not hire some from outside? After all, another great ESD, Roger Penske, had recently purchased Detroit Diesel from GM and increased its market share from 5% to 25% in just five years. An outsider ESD is much better than an insider bureaucrat.

So what's the problem? Why doesn't every company use ESDs effectively? Because ESDs drive bureaucrats nuts. Here's why:

- *ESDs trust their own judgment and love their own vision*, and when these get off track, they can be disastrous. Ford nearly went bankrupt twice because Henry refused to replace obsolete models—first the Model T and then the Model A. Why? His vision was a car for everyone—the cheapest possible functional vehicle—and for him that meant endlessly refining the production system for a single model. (He said, "The public can have my cars any color they want as long as it is black," because black paint dried faster than other paint.)

- *ESDs won't play the game*. Good bureaucrats do. Bureaucrats are properly deferential to authority. They mingle well at parties. They admire the emperor's new clothes. They make sure the procedures are followed. They avoid risk. ESDs are focused on their vision and often impatient of anything else. They are fiercely ambitious for opportunities to achieve their visions but often indifferent to promotion; one chief engineer for Corolla had been in the position for 20 years. (You can imagine how smoothly those projects run!)[14]

14. This was the author's understanding at the time of writing.

Every organization needs bureaucrats—many more bureaucrats than ESDs. Someone has to keep the ESDs from doing something crazy. Someone has to pay attention to the day-to-day details, filling in the blanks in the ESDs' visions. Someone has to smooth ruffled feathers, schmooze customers, track deliverables, and check up on the work. Someone has to build knowledge for the future and ensure commonality across projects.

ESDs usually are not very good at these functions. Their visions burn too brightly and pull them too strongly. (This is not a license for ESDs to ignore details like a coffee house artiste or demagogic politician. Details matter. It is an observation that the ESD needs to focus on the details of the future value stream; not the details of keeping track of who goes on vacation when.) For best results, ESDs need a smoothly running machine manned by bureaucrats.

Every company is started and built by an ESD, who hires bureaucrats to make things work. As soon as the ESD dies, the bureaucrats heave a sigh of relief: *"Thank God. At last we'll be able to get some peace and order around here."* They believe that they can perform the ESD's job: *"Create a vision—how hard is that?"* But the visions are insipid or impossible, and the "peace and order" (actually confusion and disorder) spread until finally the organization drowns in its own bureaucracy.

Kiirchiro Toyoda's greatest achievement may simply have been to recognize that he was an ESD, not a bureaucrat. He hired a bureaucrat to run the company while he focused on creating systems. Toyota has continued to tolerate ESDs and use ESDs ever since. Taiichi Ohno is the most famous—and few successful men have been more hated by their contemporaries. The first auto project leader at Toyota had been a great designer of manufacturing systems but was so abrasive that no one dared to actually have the project team work for him. The second had designed fighter planes—a deeply integrated system—and was a more cheerful individual, who wrote in instructions for future chief engineers that the project leader must get along with the department heads. Thus was born the current system of constant tension between department leaders and project leaders—a profoundly creative tension in which each needs the other.

That is the tension your organization must achieve. The tension between ESDs and more technically specialized and bureaucratic department heads pulls the organization forward and keeps it on track. Conflict leads to information exchange, which leads to consensus. Conflicts between an ESD and a working developer can be carried up the chain of support to a departmental manager of equal rank, who works out the compromise with the ESD.

Said one Toyota chief engineer: "Lot's of conflict makes a great car." Yet, said one Toyota general manager: "We can always work out a compromise." How is this possible?

Project leaders and department heads understand their roles, and how they need each other. Both know they can turn their ideas into steel only through each other.

The project leader has the technical respect of the departments as a proven, creative engineer. If project leaders and equally ranked departmental leaders cannot arrive at agreement—if they have to "take the problem upstairs"—both normally are seen as incompetent. ESDs have a direct line to the company president and demand and get the support of every function. A function can argue with the ESD only through evidence that the chief engineer is making a mistake that would hurt the company.

If compromise cannot be reached, the department must support the ESD. As a symbol of this, a Toyota chief engineer signs every drawing. All discussions are placed in a common frame of reference—earning higher profit by reducing cost or better serving the customer. The chief engineer has to find a solution that really works; there are no excuses for failure.

This system—total system design responsibility by the project leader, total supervision responsibility by functional managers—has several advantages:

- It frees the project leader to focus on system design. (The extremely simple project management tools discussed under "pull and flow management" also help.)

- It ensures highly skilled day-to-day technical supervision.

- It provides a balance between the natural tendency of developers to focus all their attention on the project at hand, and the need to accumulate knowledge and create consistency across projects.

- It makes major mistakes nearly impossible because the departmental experts will rein in any project leader taking excessive risks.

ESDs must generate inspiring, sharply focused visions in order to draw the support of working developers they must lead, not command.

The ESDs can break down communication barriers between departments, demanding effective communications.

To make this work, however, the company president must always look first to the ESDs —the only people other than the president who are responsible for profit. Unless they have vigorous support from the top, the far larger number of bureaucrats will bury them.

Now how will your company pick and train project leaders?

Picking and developing lean project and business leaders

Good system-designer entrepreneurs have the following characteristics:

- *They want the job*. They have a burning desire to create new products and value streams. They are eager to take responsibility and be held accountable. If they perform well, their usual reward is the opportunity to do it some more.

- *They already have designed systems*—integrating a complete project of some kind.

- *They learn fast, technically and otherwise*. They have a profound grasp of engineering and economic fundamentals. They can communicate with and earn the respect of technologists of all kinds.

- *They like getting their hands dirty*—but are able to back away from the details and focus on the big picture.

- *They have good judgment*. They need to make a lot of decisions, most of them with incomplete data. They will need to override the beliefs of experts. (Marketing studies on the 1984 Taurus predicted disaster. Veraldi held fast and changed the public's taste.)

- *They can visualize the whole system that they want to create.*

- *They communicate their vision of the product and value stream*; and they can listen effectively to every member of the team.

- *They can work the informal systems of the company*—the ones that actually get things done.

- *They have good technical and business intuitions.*

Intuition is not mystical. Far less than 1% of the brain processing power reaches the level of conscious thought. Every successful activity is performed mostly unconsciously or intuitively. Consciousness is just too slow. Said one Toyota vice president for development: "Often intuition is better than engineering." When Kelly Johnson and the Lockheed skunkworks were designing the SR-71 to fly at 3,000 miles per hour, the thermal modeling engineer projected that air temperatures at the engine inlets would reach 750 degrees. Johnson bet him a case of beer they would be 700. They came in at 720. But notice that they still did the model. Intuition must guide analysis but is too unreliable to replace it.

Notice that this has very little to do with any particular engineering or business discipline. Pick the person, not the paper qualifications, and don't worry if they are missing some technical or business skills; if you pick the right people, they'll learn fast.

I need to emphasize again that while this is a combined technical, leadership, and commercial responsibility, it is system-design skill—the ability to integrate the entire value stream—that inspires followers and accomplishes the commercial mission. Some successful project leaders lack technical skills—but they are usually only successful once or twice because they are relying on unusual relationships in the development team to substitute for their own skills. Conversely, many system-oriented engineers can quickly learn the needed business skills.

Again, good ESDs often have trouble in a bureaucracy and in school. (My most impressive student at the University of Michigan couldn't go on to Michigan's graduate school because he had a 3.2 GPA. He said, "I'm here to learn, and getting a 4.0 would take too much time." But he had, as a sophomore, written a computer program that earned him $100,000.) Toyota claims to prefer "B" students.

Lesson: You can't pick ESDs by grade point or bureaucratic personnel evaluations. But how will you recognize them? It's easy. Get out of your office and talk to engineers about their projects. (Include their personal projects. The stuff they are doing at home.)

The potential ESDs will:

- Have ideas, about everything.
- Be enthusiastic, proud, excited, and even angry.
- Clearly connect engineering decisions with business needs.
- See beyond their part of the project, and find win-win solutions.
- Quickly understand and build on critiques.
- Explain clearly what they are doing, and why.

To confirm, check on their past performance. Do their decisions work out? Do they stick around long enough to make things work? You will have to look at actual results and multiple sources of information; watch out for bosses who feel threatened. Henry Ford had been fired from almost every job he held before starting Ford because he kept telling his bosses what to do.

Above all, look at their work. Mozart is famous for his music, not his appearance, social skills, or political savvy. You are looking for people who can simultaneously compose a vision of a great value stream and orchestrate the realization of that value stream. The best evidence they can do it is that they have done it, and they want to do it again.

Having identified potential ESDs, smart companies develop them. First, make sure they understand some area of engineering thoroughly. They have to know what real expertise is so that they can recognize it. Then, give them increasingly broad and varied project assignments. If you have small projects, have them start small, but assign more experienced ESDs to mentor them. If you have big projects only, make them assistants to the project leader. Shield them from the bureaucracy, and let them develop some personal flair—but hold them responsible for results.

Many potential ESDs will reach a level at which they are incompetent. That is O.K. You can convert them back into specialist departmental engineering leaders, or give them smaller projects within their limits.

Be careful in converting conventional project leaders to ESDs. Some of them were always frustrated ESDs and will do fine. Others did well in a conventional environment because they were good at tracking tasks and deliverables and at nicely asking people to hurry up; they may fail completely as ESDs. Many potential ESDs will have chosen to stick to straight design engineering, believing (correctly) that they would be bored silly by the bureaucratic and political load on a conventional project leader. You will have to convince them this will be different.

You may not need full-fledged ESDs for every project. Many projects aren't very creative; they involve minor changes to an existing product to satisfy a new customer, which must be shepherded through the system but which don't require a new vision. You may be best off having these run by the salesperson responsible for the customer because they have a powerful incentive to get the project through successfully. Or simply assign an engineer to take charge.

So what if you looked around, and can't find enough people to do the job now while you develop future ESDs? Hire them from outside. Your organization badly needs the shake-up anyway.

A final warning. Good system-design entrepreneurs are primarily motivated by the desire to create, not the desire for promotion—but they become frustrated by seeing promotions given to those they don't respect. Many conventional companies rapidly promote those who give great presentations, flatter their bosses, and move rapidly enough to escape the consequences of their decisions. ESDs tend to leave these companies. The only appropriate criterion for promoting departmental managers is their effective support of ESDs over a prolonged period.

The rest of this section will change viewpoints. So far, we've been talking about what the company should do. Now, let's think about what the ESD project leader should do.

What would you do if it were yours?

O.K., you're a project leader. Now what? Everyone in the company is yanking you a different direction. Marketing wants impossible specifications. The engineering procedures office has a million checklists for you to fill out. You can't get the resources you need from product engineering, and the manufacturing engineers are so busy with current production problems that they won't even talk to you. You've hardly started, and it looks like you are already behind schedule. Advanced Development handed you a concept you don't believe in. There is a long list of standard tasks for you and the team to accomplish, but you have a sneaking fear that the end result is going to have serious problems. It's been years since the company launched a product on time, in budget, and without serious quality problems. Purchasing wants a ton of paper before they will even go look for a supplier, and then they go with the lower bidder—who has no design-in capability even if you could get them soon enough to design in. And your boss wants you to take responsibility for three different projects. What do you do?

First, set up a cycle. Work on each project for two hours a day, or one day a week, leaving slack time to spend where it seems most useful. Don't go nuts about this, but try to stabilize things as much as you reasonably can.

Then, take a deep breath and make a decision. Can you really perform the ESD role without unacceptable risk to your career? Do you have enough skills, and can you get enough help, to pull it off? Do you want to? If the answer to all questions is yes, ask yourself another question. What would you do if it were your money? What would you do if project failure would cost you your house, and success would make you rich? You can use that trick throughout the project. Very likely, the first answer would be to get with the customers.

Representing customers

We asked a Toyota engineer how he knows what customers want: "The chief engineer tells me," he responded. The chief engineer for the Avalon is said to have spent a month living with a California family to understand U.S. customers better. Why? Isn't it marketing's job to represent the customer?

One Toyota vice president for development has answered the question. Market research is too conservative. It can only represent customer needs as the customer currently understands them. But the system designer can look beneath the surface to see how an innovative system can change the way customers understand and satisfy their needs.

Marketing can help though. If you sell to a mass market, they can gather data much more broadly than you can and help you to understand it. If you are a supplier to only a few companies, sales should be able to get you in the door and tell you who to talk to. Be flattering, be interested, be deferential, but be clear: You intend to understand the customer's needs in detail and take responsibility for meeting them.

You need the knowledge of the customer and general recognition that you speak for the customer in order to hold your own in conflict with the departments. Of course, you need to be honest in reporting what the customer wants, but if you are honest and you really know, you will have a tremendous advantage in negotiating.

Representing the customer means that you cannot accept specifications defined by other people—even the customer. Customers may or may not know what they want, but they certainly don't know what you can do, so they can't set sound specifications. As we'll see later, lean development relies on flexible targets rather than rigid specifications anyway—but setting targets is part of creating the vision, and you have to do it yourself.

If you are selling to industrial customers, try to get out in front of them. Gather data about their needs from any source you can find—especially operating and testing their equipment. Present them with a vision or ideas or, best of all, prototypes, and get their reaction. Then, tell them you are refining the vision by presenting targets to them.

Explain that you'd like to keep some flexibility in the targets, but that you will try to achieve more, not less (and be conservative enough that you can do it). Try hard to show them actual performance data and see if it is good enough, rather than pinning down the exact requirements ahead of time. But above all, be sure that you actually understand their needs as well as you possibly can; more projects have failed for delivering the wrong product than for any other reason.

If you are selling to the government, it is even harder. Until recently, U.S. government bureaucracies (at least, the Dept. of Defense) weren't comfortable buying anything unless they had previously written a specification for it. That is changing, and you may find competitive advantage in getting further out in front. (Nor was meeting the specification ever a guarantee of project success; many a project met the spec but was canceled because the spec didn't really make sense.)

The biggest trick in getting in front of the customer may be getting in front of your own sales department. Sales often sells "vaporware"—so your first connection with your project may be after someone has put in a quote. Try hard not to let this happen; form a working relationship with the salespeople. (You have something to offer them: Industrial customers usually are happier talking to a project leader than a salesperson.) If possible, start forming your vision and selling it to your own company before anyone else can screw it up—the subject of the next section.

Negotiating for resources, agreeing on the vision

I've lumped these together because you usually have to do them at the same time. Of course, what you'd really like is to be handed all the resources you might need before the project even starts; have them working for you full time; and drop the ones who turn out not to fit into your vision as you create it. Good luck! What you will really get is a fraction of a person here and there, most of whom will be very skeptical about your vision. So how do you get the team—and just as important their bosses—to support you?

You have to get them excited about the vision. Vision is like the pencil sketch a painter puts on the canvas before beginning with oils, or like the basic melody around which a composer creates a symphony. It provides direction, it unifies the effort—and, it has to be beautiful and coherent already. The vision starts out very simple and rough and may go through several versions. As it is modified, it gradually gains detail and solves problems until it isn't a vision anymore but rather a partially completed value stream. At that point, if you've done a good job, you are over the hump. The rest is filling things in.

You assemble your vision out of many inputs. Talk to customers, suppliers, plants, research labs. Work with industrial designers, marketers, and engineers. Subsystem development in lean companies proceeds continuously rather than waiting for projects, so there should be new technologies, or at least ideas, you can draw on.

As you talk to people, explain your ideas. Be open and flexible: "*I'm not sure whether to do this or that; what do you think?*" During this process you will gather a lot more ideas, and you will find which developers you want on the team. (Try to get a sense of how heavily they are loaded, too; no point in asking for someone who is grossly over-loaded.)

Look for innovations everywhere in marketing approach, in supplied components, and especially in manufacturing. Don't worry yet about trying too many new things; the problem isn't considering new things, it's committing to them before they are proven, and we'll see how to deal with that later.

Talk to their managers: "*I'm doing the preliminary thinking about a project to double our sales of automatic fish gutters. I need to bounce some ideas off a manufacturing engineer. Got a creative one, who might be available to work on the project when it gets going? And, by the way, can I show you what I'm thinking?*" You want them to be excited, and you want them to have ownership, so you can get the support you need.

Your basic negotiating ploy is simple: *"Given support A, I can do X. Given support B, I think I can only do Y. X makes 50% more money for the company."* (We'll talk later about how to make this claim.)

Your goal is a brief written document (mostly pictures) and a briefing, exciting enough, complete enough, and realistic enough to pull the project members forward—getting them excited and allowing them to decide for themselves whether they are going in the right direction or not. Allow management to make the key initial investment decision—to formally form the team and launch the project.

Here's what you need to put in it: First, describe the customers and their unique, new, or most important needs, as well as other critical factors in the situation. Tie these to a succinct statement of the intent for the product. Here is an imaginary example for a real product, the Toyota Tundra pickup, introduced in 2000.

FYI: Background and customer needs

Americans love big, powerful machines. Even American women seem to have fallen in love with vehicles no Japanese could park, partly because there are so many on the road that driving a small vehicle feels unsafe. SUVs and light trucks comprise about half of the U.S. market and almost all the profits in that market.

Toyota has not been a major player in this market. This was partly for lack of large engines and partly out of fear that a successful vehicle built in Japan would trigger American protectionism. Now, Toyota is creating the capacity to build both the trucks and a suitable engine in the U.S. At the same time, Americans are concerned about rising fuel prices and declining reliability, and again appear willing to buy Japanese-designed trucks, particularly if they are built in the U.S.

Therefore, Tundra will be a large, powerful-feeling machine, but with Toyota sophistication and reliability. It will aim at the center of the pickup market, with styling and road handling that appeals to both men and women. It will provide a platform for further generations of SUVs and be an ideal "large Yuppie truck," but we will provide versions suitable for off-road enthusiasts and the construction market. If market tastes change back toward cars, these variants will ensure a reasonable return on our investment. If the general public continues to buy large, truck-type vehicles, we will become as dominant in that market as we are in small, mid-sized, and luxury sedans.

Supplement your intent statement with *sketches*, especially if you are selling a styled product. Then get down to *targets*. Provide a matrix of the characteristics of competitive products price, performance, weight, reliability, etc. Show the targets for your envisioned product as intervals where appropriate—"120–130 horsepower"; you don't know yet exactly where you will wind up.

Show the *system architecture*. What are the major subsystems, and how do they fit together? What is the basic design philosophy—for a truck, body on frame, or some innovative, more integrated structural design? What alternatives are you considering for the major subsystems? Are you considering four bar, trailing link, cross beam, or MacPherson strut suspensions? What manufacturing innovations are you considering? Why have you discarded other options? Make decisions if you have the data; leave them partially open if you don't. Stick to the tried and true unless something else is significantly better. This makes design, debugging and manufacturing easier; a senior GM body engineer tells me that every Toyota sedan uses the same basic scheme for creating torsional rigidity.

Cover the entire *value stream*. Where will the product be built? Why? What key suppliers do you expect to use, and why? Show an alignment map.

Provide a *feasibility analysis*. Do some "back-of-the-envelope" calculations. Analyze historical data. Do some quick and dirty experiments if needed.

List the *resources* you need, and a brief *schedule* of target events such as launch and prototype builds. (You'll learn more about target events when we discuss cadence, pull, and flow.)

Show the *expected profit* model.

Then *summarize*.

Let me emphasize again the system vision is the most critical test of the system designer's judgment and experience. Although the "set-based" approach allows you to wait for data on more issues than a conventional approach would, you still are making the most critical decisions of the design right now. You need to do good analysis, study the historical record, and think very carefully.

An example illustrates why analysis of the vision is so important. NASA's space shuttle was designed around the basic architectural decision to make it land like an airplane, with all major systems reusable. This vision was compelling, exciting, and wrong. It now is clear that parachutes and airbags could have produced a much lighter and more economical recovery system, and that reducing the production cost for rocket components would have been much easier than refurbishing reusable ones. Pounds delivered to orbit by the shuttle are much more expensive than pounds delivered by conventional rocket, and the U.S. accordingly lost launch business to foreign competitors. Worst, calculations made at the time accurately projected this. They were ignored, and the author of the analysis fired because the airplane image was intuitively so attractive.

One probably could tell similar stories about any number of Internet startups in the late 1990s. System designers whose visions work rightly are seen as heroes; those whose visions turn out to conflict with physics and economics do enormous harm. Test your vision as well as you can; don't get swept away by buzzwords.

You want everyone who will work on the project, and their bosses, to agree to the vision. How to achieve this, and how much detail you'll have in the vision at the agreement point, varies a lot from company to company:

At Toyota, the vision is assembled by the ESD, consulting with others, over a period ranging from years down to perhaps three months. ESDs then brief the vision to all the people who will work on the project, then to their fellow project leaders, and finally to the president and board of directors. At each stage they meet opposition and suggestions. The project leader strives for consensus, persuading others of the value of the vision, while incorporating knowledge and creativity. At the end of the briefing, the company president approves the project—with its budget.

At Honda, the large-project leader takes a core team of perhaps 60 leading developers offsite for about two months to formulate the vision and a fairly detailed system concept.

At Denso, the entire team contributes to the formation of loose targets, but they delay architectural decisions in order to allow more room for innovation during the project.

If possible, get your whole budget approved at the vision briefing to senior management, subject of course to modification if required. Conventional companies often delay the most important investment decision—to invest in tooling—until after the design is complete. In lean companies, however, tooling development should often begin almost immediately, so the tooling investment decision can be made at the beginning. Then, it is up to the project leader to try to beat the budget, finding ways to save money that can be anticipated at the start. (If instead there are problems that force spending more money, then something is wrong: The project leader is inexperienced, or the system is forcing over-optimistic estimates.)

Taking responsibility for profit and risk

How do you pull cooperation from departmental leaders? How do you decide where to put your resources?

Staying in close touch with customers and senior executives is part of the story. Another part is learning the language of project profit and project risk. Back in Part 1, we saw how to estimate both risk and profit. I recommend also that you prepare the more sophisticated profit models taught by Reinertsen in *Managing the Design Factory*.

Here's another useful tool: the profit-based decision matrix. I've seen too many project teams waste months on concepts that the crudest profit analysis would have eliminated immediately, so use profit-based decision matrices early and often. The example covers a decision on the body architecture of a car.

	A	B	C	D	E
1	**Decision: body architecture**		base case: frame		
2	**Alternatives ▶**	monocoque		hybrid	
3	**Criterion ▼**	profit change	uncertainty	profit change	uncertainty
4	manufacturing cost	-50	8	-30	5
5	handling	30	8	10	5
6	noise	30	8	10	5
7	Totals	10	14	-10	9

The decision matrix analyzes alternatives against a base case—here, the use of a frame. Column A shows the criteria for evaluating the other alternatives against the base case. Columns B and D then show how much more or less money per car we would expect to make as a result of using that alternative, considering only the listed criteria. For example, a monocoque design would cost $50 per car more than the frame design, but we estimate that the average customer would pay $30 more for the improved handling, and another $30 for the reduced noise.

Columns C and E are the real trick. They show the uncertainty in our estimates. For the hybrid design, we are 90% certain that our profit change estimates are within $5 of the real number; for the monocoque, the uncertainty per criterion is $8.

The total uncertainty is the square root of the sum of the squares. In this case, the monocoque design looks best with a $10 improvement over the base case. But, we are confident of our numbers only within a $14 uncertainty; we should gather more data. On the other hand, we have better than a 90% certainty that the hybrid is worse than the base case; we can stop wasting time on it.

This simple tool often resolves issues in an hour that teams have been arguing about for months. But don't let people sidetrack you into using "points" instead of dollars. You can spend forever arguing about how many points to assign and how to weight them. Use dollars. You know what they mean.

Finally, don't allow your boss or a functional manager to make decisions for you. Draw on their knowledge, decide how much you believe their intuitions—but take responsibility for your own decisions. Do the best, most objective profitability analysis you can, and stick to them. Fight for your right to approve suppliers, designs, manufacturing processes, budgets, launch dates, customer, and specifications. Lead your business.

Taking responsibility for profit is a tough job. You won't get all the support you want. Manufacturing engineers and purchasing representatives likely will give you much less time, flexibility, and creativity than you want. Product engineers will be difficult to constrain to designing something manufacturable and therefore profitable. Purchasing may insist on its responsibility for part costs and supplier decisions. The comptroller's office may demand that you "prove" your project will be profitable (as if proof were possible). Marketing may insist that they know what the customer wants—or worse, confess to having no idea. Your boss may want to make key decisions. You will spend your life negotiating, explaining, and listening.

So, read the material in this book (at least) on win-win negotiation. And take advantage of your most powerful tool: you as the system designer.

Designing the system

System design is the primary source of your power and your project's success. But what do you actually do? What does "design the system" mean, anyway?

You probably have your own ideas, but here are a few basics. These concepts apply as soon as you start working on the project and continue to apply through launch; system design is a skill, not a phase.

First, clearly identify the main questions your project must answer. The specialists on your team will define questions in terms of their specialties; you must keep them focused on the real questions.

Here's an example. Some years ago I reviewed the Army's Unmanned Ground Vehicle (UGV) programs. I predicted none would produce a tactically useful system, and none did. Why? Partly because of a law of physics.

To make sense, UGVs should be smaller than manned vehicles. If the vehicle is big enough for a man, you can always enhance performance by putting one on board.

However, as size decreases, so does the ability to crush through off-road obstacles. This is because the strength of objects increases as the square of their linear dimensions, but their weight increases as the cube. So, strength-to-weight ratio is inversely proportional to size. (A one-inch cube of medium-strength steel weighs 0.3 pounds, and can support 100,000 pounds, 330,000 times its own weight. A 10-inch cube weighs 300 pounds and can support 10 million pounds, 33,000 times its own weight. That's why ants can carry many times their own weight.) Therefore, in relation to their weight, small vehicles face stronger obstacles than large vehicles. So, tanks can smash their way across terrain that is totally impassable to small vehicles.

Therefore, the first issue associated with military unmanned ground vehicles is whether or not they actually have any battlefield use. A good system designer would have started with simple field trials using small manned vehicles to simulate unmanned vehicles. The Army's technical specialists framed the question as, *"Can we build unmanned ground vehicles?"* But the more important question is, *"Would unmanned ground vehicles do any good?"*

So, your first challenge as a system designer is to make sure the team is working on the right problems. The right problems usually are simpler than the problems the specialists want to work on, and usually are tied very directly to customer needs.

Second, shape and innovate the overall system architecture. What are the basic underlying concepts? (Automobiles can be built around frames or a stressed skin concept; machine tools can derive precision from structural rigidity or advanced feedback controls.) What are the major subsystems? How are they arranged? What allowance will you give each subsystem, for space, weight, and cost?

Focus on the way things fit together; look for opportunities for major gains by re-arranging or recombining the subsystems. The DC-3 was the first successful commercial airliner in part because it combined existing design concepts—twin engines, all-metal monocoque construction, and movable flaps—for the first time. Ford put together the automobile, the conveyor belt, and the assembly line. Kiirchiro Toyoda combined the concepts of craftsmanship, industrial engineering, and mass production of interchangeable parts in a new way. He held the craftsmen responsible for using the techniques of industrial engineering to improve their own processes for mass production.

(Conversely, U.S. car companies abandoned craftsmanship in favor of mass production controlled by industrial engineers, while some European companies maintained the craft tradition and still have not completely achieved part interchangeability.)[15]

Use visual tools. In aircraft design, for example, the system designer draws the airplane. Most Toyota chief engineers communicate their concepts in sketches; stylists and body engineers work out the complete picture. Function-block diagrams help for electrical and mechanical systems. Flow charts can help visualize logic. Alignment maps and manufacturing value-stream maps (*Leaning to See*, Shook and Rother) can help you visualize the entire value stream. Finite state machine models can be very useful for some software systems.

Shape the architecture around the fundamental factors driving the design. Aircraft are smoothly curved for aerodynamics. The 3,000-mile-per-hour SR-71 reconnaissance plane is designed entirely around the need for speed—the fuel tanks leak until air friction heats and tightens the structure!

15. This was the author's understanding at the time of writing.

Houses are rectangular for ease in allocating volume. Geodesic domes therefore are bad system design for middle-class American housing. But domes are good design for igloos—igloo design is driven by weakness in tension of the only available building material, snow; the dome keeps the whole structure in compression.

Keep it simple. Good architectures have direct and simple connections between cause and effect. Operation is intuitive, without surprises. The flows of energy, stress, and intuition are as short as possible. There are no extra parts. Subsystems fit cleanly, without unneeded connections or overlaps. Compare the structure of good hand tools with the Rube Goldberg cartoons. Microsoft Excel is a good product because, despite the best efforts of Microsoft to ruin it, its fundamental simplicity makes it useful for many purposes. Microsoft Word, in my opinion, is a weaker product because its excess of bells and whistles makes it unreliable and unpredictable, and subtly guide the user toward a particular style of writing.

Allocate every subsystem enough space, weight, and cost, but not too much. Do a cost breakdown, allocating a cost to every subsystem. Leave some flex in these targets at the system boundaries and emphasize the value of beating the targets.

Third, define consistent technical philosophies. Have the team solve the same problems in the same way throughout the system. For example according to a Polaroid engineer, one Polaroid camera was a terrible system design. It had 70 different kinds of fasteners! The return rate was above 100%—many cameras were returned twice. I have built a number of machines that used only one fastener, a 1/4-20 socket head cap screw.

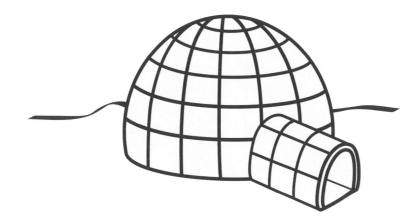

Ease of assembly and maintenance was far more important for these one-off machines than adding a little weight and cost (when the screw was too big, or drilling a few extra holes when the screw was too small).

Strive for harmony between the parts of the system and the super-system in which it will be used. A fast-looking car should have handling and power to match. An economical engine should be economical to maintain and get good gas mileage. A high-performance spark plug should have better-than-usual heat tolerance as well as fouling resistance. A stereo designed to provide the absolute limit of precision for classical music should have conservative styling and elegant controls. A stereo designed for maximum volume at minimum price should be colorful and aggressive in appearance. A luxury product should not rely on the cheapest possible suppliers.

You will base these decisions on your target customers, but consistency is more important than hitting the target. A coherently designed product will appeal to someone; a hodgepodge of conflicting decisions will annoy everyone.

Fourth, eliminate weak points, make sound trade-off decisions, and address threats to success. Great systems are "tough" or "balanced"; they often are surprisingly effective in roles for which they were not originally designed. The F-16 fighter plane originally was designed as a low-cost lightweight good weather "air supremacy" fighter, but it has expanded into a wide variety of roles in part because the basic design is so well balanced. Conversely, the Japanese WWII Zero fighter would have been a great system design except for its inability to absorb damage, largely because it lacked self-sealing fuel tanks.

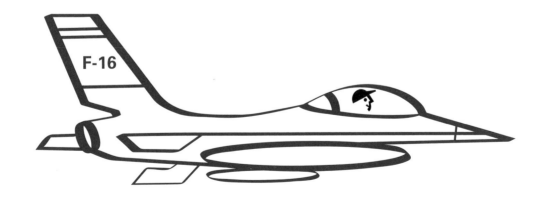

Fifth, manage the development process to produce the innovations, integration knowledge, and feasibility information you need. That's why you're the project leader—to make the development process serve system design. And of course, the development process is a system, so all of your system-design skills apply to designing the development process itself.

We'll discuss how to distill many alternatives into one in the section on set-based concurrent engineering. The section on cadence, pull, and flow will tell you how to plan and control events with a minimum of bureaucracy and a maximum of flexibility. The section on teams of responsible experts will tell you how to work toward consensus within the team.

Finally, in the words of one Toyota chief engineer—project leader and entrepreneur system designer—"This is the best job in Toyota. I take $100 million and 1,000 people, and I make a car." Have fun!

 DO

Implement entrepreneur system designer leadership

Start experimental projects using ESDs. This lets you experiment with the whole system without changing the whole organization at once. Carefully pick these first few project leaders. Just make sure they are volunteers, and give them enough freedom and support to do the job. Have them meet once a month or quarter with the company's senior executives and report what they have learned.

There is one major difference between ESDs in a lean company and the ESDs who start companies. ESDs inside a company don't get rich, even if the project succeeds. Therefore, it is unfair to make them take the kinds of risks routinely taken by company founders. Conventional companies therefore diffuse responsibility, letting project leaders off the hook of responsibility for profit. Lean companies instead provide project leaders with a development approach that almost always works—set-based concurrent engineering.

Set-based concurrent engineering (SBCE)

How can you:

- Satisfy many kinds of customers from a single project?

- Innovate without risk, ensuring that every project leaps ahead of the competition?

- Learn rapidly and apply this learning effectively to future projects?

- Achieve highly optimized, well-integrated systems?

- Achieve complete concurrency in the design of manufacturing systems and products, systems, and subsystems?

- Reuse manufacturing systems and parts?

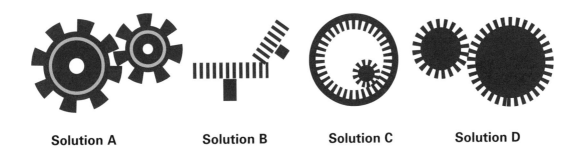

| **Solution A** | **Solution B** | **Solution C** | **Solution D** |

By replacing conventional development with set-based concurrent engineering, or SBCE. In SBCE, the design team:

- Simultaneously explores *multiple solutions* for every subsystem of both product and manufacturing system.

- Aggressively attacks those solutions with *rapid, low-cost analysis and tests*, progressively eliminating weak solutions.

- Uses the results of analysis and tests to create a *trade-off curve knowledge base* that defines the limits of the possible.

- Converges on a solution only after it has been proven.

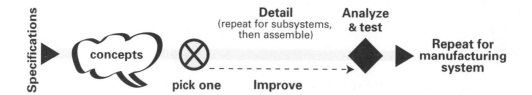

FYI

Conventional development works roughly like this:

1. Someone (usually Marketing or the customer) defines specifications for the product.

2. A brainstorming effort produces a number of possible concepts.

3. The team quickly picks a concept. (Often, the fundamental concept is chosen during advanced development or proposal writing, before the project even begins.)

4. The team "details" the concept, providing specifications to subsystems. Each subsystem design team repeats the whole process.

5. The team tests the subsystems. (This is sometimes called "V-shaped" development, working from top-down during design, and bottom-up during testing.)

6. The team tests the system.

7. (Optional): A few companies build in time to iteratively improve the concept after evaluation. But late-concept changes almost always are disastrous, so most programs stay close to the initial idea, or are canceled.

8. The entire process is repeated for the manufacturing system.

This model carries a powerful emotional appeal. Many variations have been published, and it has been greatly detailed in thousands of development process manuals. Unfortunately, it contains a fundamental flaw: The development team decides on the approach they will use before they know it is the best or even whether it will work at all.

As a result, the learnings-to-costs ratio is low. Recall that the learnings-to-costs ratio is:

$$\frac{\text{integration (especially customer) learning X innovation X feasibility learning}}{\text{cost X time X risk}}$$

More precisely:

- The team picks the fundamental concept based on old data, since the project has not had time to generate much new data. This forces either high risk or low innovation.

- The team tests one concept per design cycle—this is slow. A complete system has to be built and tested for each learning—this is expensive. Worse, since no one can interpolate between one datum, the learning is not very useful for future designs.

The specifications are decided at the beginning of the project, on the basis of old knowledge. Every specification is a trade-off between what really is wanted and what the state of the art allows. At the beginning of the project, only the old state of the art is known, so the team must guess what the state of the art will be at the end of the project. Such guesses usually are wrong and produce designs that are over-stressed in some ways and under-challenged in others. Further, customers' wants are based on their experience with old products. How can they know they want new product features until someone invents them?

- System decisions are made on the basis of old component knowledge—or by guessing at what future component innovations may be possible. This makes total system optimization nearly impossible. Some subsystems are over-stressed while others get off easy.

- Product design decisions are made on basis of knowledge of the old manufacturing system. The old knowledge often is too constraining, so product designers bet on future manufacturing innovation. This often pushes the manufacturing system to the "bleeding edge," precluding re-use and setting up quality problems. And there is little manufacturing innovation until product designers demand it, so product designers don't get the opportunity to do the really interesting things that new manufacturing processes might allow.

- Chaos—scatter caused by expediting—is the norm. Time is short because so much—system and component design, product and manufacturing system design—has to happen in sequence. But timing is unpredictable because the model relies on iteration to deal with problems.

These problems are built into this approach to development and can't be changed just by pushing for concurrent engineering. Studies show that the concurrent engineering movement has had little impact in the United States.

In fact, without a set-based process, real concurrency between product and manufacturing system development, let alone system and component design, is almost impossible.

If product designers look at only one solution at a time, then change that solution when they run into problems, manufacturing system designers are forced to run behind them, making changes as they go. The manufacturing engineers soon decide that they are better off waiting until the product designers make up their minds—and they are back to critiquing product designs on the basis of old information.

Component designers have the same motive to wait for system design. Worse, if system designers rely on concurrent innovation in component design, they may be forced to scrap their entire concepts when the component innovation fails.

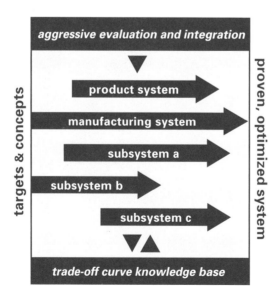

SBCE counters all these problems. It works like this:

1. The team breaks the system down into subsystems and sub-subsystems, into the smallest pieces feasible.

2. They identify broad targets for the system and each subsystem.

3. They create multiple concepts for the system and each subsystem, including both product and manufacturing systems.

4. They filter these concepts by aggressive evaluation, identifying failure modes and finding failure points for each. They also filter by integration, eliminating concepts that don't fit with each other, the customer's needs (preferably as expressed after seeing what is possible), the competitive situation, etc.

5. Failure information goes into a *trade-off curve* knowledge base that guides the design. Trade-off curves describe the limits of performance that are possible with a given design approach.

6. As they filter, they increase the accuracy, detail, and cost of the concept models and tests. They tune the rate of convergence, the rate of detailing, and the level of innovation so that the last concept standing is well proven and optimized.

trade-off curve for a family of mufflers

Thus, SBCE decisions are based on data. Said one Toyota general manager: "Everyone —suppliers, engineers—wants to make the decision and get on with the project. The manager's job is to keep people from making decisions before they have the data."

SBCE dramatically increases the learnings-to-costs ratio by:

- *Using redundancy to reduce risk* the same way redundancy reduces risk in multi-engine aircraft: If one concept fails, another takes over. We'll see later how to calculate the risk reduction, which usually is a factor of 5 to 10. Properly executed, SBCE almost guarantees successful products and manufacturing systems, on time and in budget. This dramatically reduces the expediting scatter associated with canceled projects, last minute fixes, and rush projects to catch up with a competitor.

- *Increasing innovation by giving more ideas adequate detail and evaluation.* One team increased patent applications 10 times.

- *Letting you schedule innovation*: Denso, for example, regularly imposes deadlines and selects customers for projects aimed at producing strategic breakthroughs. Conventional organizations work on one innovation at a time; since there is no way of knowing whether the idea will work out, success can't be scheduled. But lean organizations know that some kind of innovation always is possible in any technical area within given constraints of time and budget, and they scan a number of possibilities to find that innovation.

Testing earlier in the development process when it is much cheaper. For example, Toyota builds a lot of early prototypes, checking for how well the concepts under consideration fit together. They usually need only one or two copies of these prototypes, and many aspects of the prototypes can be quite crude. Later, during the main prototype builds, Toyota typically builds only 30 copies, versus as many as several hundred for a conventional company. At $500,000 per prototype, this adds up.[16]

- *Evaluating multiple alternatives, which produces trade-off curves.* These show the limits of feasibility, even for designs that haven't been tested. This trade-off curve knowledge base allows lean companies to design for success, rather than designing using only general knowledge and hoping that the test process will "pass" the design. For example, Toyota typically does not run durability tests on prototype vehicles because the trade-off curve system ensures that the vehicles

16. This was the author's understanding at the time of writing.

all will pass. Instead, Toyota tests cheap production vehicles for durability in order to refine the trade-off curves. This is the only way to meet modern standards of quality. It isn't possible to test enough parts to assure quality.

- *Producing "conceptually robust" subsystem concepts.* Conceptually robust concepts for a subsystem work well in a wide variety of systems; they are relatively immune to variations in the rest of the system.

Each supplier and internal component department simultaneously considers a number of alternatives to serve a number of system concepts. They eliminate concepts that work in only a few specialized cases and focus on solutions that they can use everywhere. If robust enough, these become building blocks used in every system, producing standardization without standards. So, even though the organization continually is trying to re-invent everything, most concepts are re-used. (All Toyota sedans are said to use essentially the same methods for creating torsional stiffness; all door outer panels are manufactured using four hits of the stamping dies.)

This re-use of concepts allows part re-use, reducing design, manufacturing and inventory costs, and especially debugging cost and time.

- *Determining specifications at the end of the project*, when the target narrowing is complete. This leaves lots of opportunity for integration learning during the project. Customers can see multiple concepts, which generally changes their picture of what they want. Subsystems can adjust to each other, and the system design can take advantage of opportunities created by subsystem innovation.

- *Designing the manufacturing system and product concurrently*, including both in-house and vendor-supplied subsystems. Manufacturing engineers and suppliers can offer exciting new capabilities for product engineers to exploit.

Thus, SBCE is the primary countermeasure to the wastes of wishful thinking, testing to specifications, and discarded knowledge. And it has powerful effect on the wastes of waiting and scatter.

Are you convinced? Most people at this point are torn between two different intuitions. Intuition One says that reducing project failures will increase profits. Intuition Two says that looking at more alternatives will increase costs. But we know that Toyota has low engineering costs per new model.

We'll see why, step by step. Let's start with the way SBCE makes it possible to "classify" projects to dramatically reduce the cost of serving customers.

Classifying projects: SBCE and the project portfolio

What kinds of projects should use SBCE? How will SBCE let you satisfy more customers without spending more on development? How will SBCE improve the reliability of your manufacturing systems? What should be the balance in your portfolio of projects between aggressiveness and conservatism?

Many conventional companies are caught in a trap. To gain new customers, they must develop innovative products. These products force innovation in the manufacturing system. Often, the manufacturing system operates on the "bleeding edge" of failure.

Manufacturing engineers therefore are swamped trying to make the current system work. So, the next manufacturing system also is "invented" late, and operates at "the bleeding edge." Manufacturing systems and processes proliferate, each attempting to solve one problem—but new problems keep appearing.

Some companies try to escape the trap by embracing agile manufacturing, using computer-controlled machines that can be programmed for new products quickly. This often worsens things because the computer-controlled systems are expensive and fragile.

Other companies embrace design-for-manufacture schemes. But these perpetuate the idea of designing the product first based on knowledge of the old manufacturing system. And they do nothing to satisfy multiple customers with a single concept.

Companies that are trying to become lean perform continuous improvement of manufacturing systems. But often, this traps them into endless tinkering because the basic cost of the manufacturing system has been built into the product design.

To avoid these traps, divide your development projects into four categories: tailoring, re-integration, strategic breakthrough, and research projects.

This division serves three purposes:

- Using the right combination of project types allows companies to satisfy more customers while reducing the number of different manufacturing systems that must be debugged and maintained.

- Different types of projects operate at different speeds and with different rules about innovation. Knowing the project type tells developers how to act.

- Rigorous classification discipline avoids the classic cause of cost overruns —taking on more innovation than the budget and time allow.

Let's look at these types in detail.

Key Characteristics of Major Project Categories

	Project Categories			
	Tailoring	**Strategic Breakthrough**	**Limited Innovation & Reintegration**	**Research**
Trade-off and limit curves	Use existing	Create new, or shift existing	Use existing	Create new, or shift existing
Product profitability	Required	Required	Required	Not a criterion
Manufacturing approach	Use existing technology	Process innovations expected	Use existing technology	Varies by project
Component Innovation timing	Precedes development with some tailoring	Simultaneous	Precedes development	Follows development
Product family	Within existing	Creates new	Within existing	Crosses family boundaries
Breadth of set	Very small	Very broad	Moderately broad	Driven by data needs
Focus	Targeted market breakthroughs	Vigorous product/process innovation	Speed; leveraging suppliers' prior to work	Good trade-off curves

Tailoring projects redesign the product and tooling within the constraints defined by existing trade-off curves in order to satisfy a new customer. For example, a supplier of sparkplugs may be asked to provide a new sparkplug that runs hotter than some of its existing plugs and cooler than others. This should require an insulator shape intermediate between the existing shapes. Success requires clear trade-off curves, especially from manufacturing engineering, so that the plug can be designed to work well and be economically and reliably manufactured, without having to create new knowledge.

Conventional companies often try to innovate during tailoring projects. They may take the contract without knowing whether innovation will be required. The result is usually disaster because the market is too small to justify the effort required for the new learning.

In particular, manufacturing engineering must constrain product engineers, stylists, and the sales organization. Manufacturing engineering must exercise absolute veto power to prevent innovation that takes the project outside the limits of the manufacturing system. A not-so-amusing story illustrates. A U.S. car company, hearing that Toyota always manufactured one external sheet metal part using four die hits, imposed the same constraint. Styling and body engineering designed a part that could not be done in four hits by conventional means. So, a brilliant die designer added hydraulically operated fingers to the last die to perform the final operations. On the first die tryout, the fingers extended successfully, but because of a software glitch, failed to retract. When the press opened, the fingers shattered, delaying the project by months.

Tailoring projects should be very fast and often involve only one or two people, so no formal leadership role is required. They may even be automated. Usually there is no need to explore a set of alternatives. The trade-off curves already characterize the set, and the designer simply picks the appropriate point in the design space.

The keys to success in tailoring projects are:

- Good strategic breakthrough projects to set up the opportunities.

- Rigorous adherence to defined limits.

- Manufacturing engineering policing the limits.

Strategic breakthrough projects aim at creating a new manufacturing system and family of products to support as many different customers as possible. For example, in one project, Denso developed a radiator core machine that could produce a wide range of core widths, core heights, and fin angles with minimum changeover time and no new tooling. The project also produced trade-off sheets predicting radiator performance as a function of these three variables. Denso is therefore set-up to do many radiator-tailoring projects. Radiator development is easy; tooling costs are low; and new products are built on the same machinery. There is almost no debugging any more.

Breakthrough projects make sense whenever the system is tightly integrated, so that innovation in one part requires innovation in all the rest, and the market is large enough to justify the effort. They are more difficult for complex systems than for simple ones such as radiators. Toyota, for example, conducted strategic breakthrough projects to develop the first Lexus luxury cars and the Prius hybrid-electric vehicle.

Aim your breakthrough projects at new product and manufacturing concepts that will provide a competitive advantage for years into the future. To do this:

- Assign your best ESD to lead the team and provide adequate resources and support from top executives. Good strategic breakthrough projects are more likely to assure the success of your company than any number of mergers or corporate re-invention programs.

- Set a launch date, with real products, real customers, and a real plant. Strategic breakthrough is not research or advanced development; it's real development.

- Map out the range of possible customer needs, extrapolated into the future. For example, the Denso team plotted the range of radiator sizes and heat transfer capacities for all of Denso's customers. And, they plotted performance versus weight over the past two decades, extending the curve a decade out to establish their own performance objectives. Then, they designed to cover most of customer needs, ignoring a few outliers.

- Innovate manufacturing in parallel with product, narrowing in on product concepts that are easy to manufacture and manufacturing concepts that support a wide range of products. The Denso team simultaneously considered a wide variety of a manufacturing and product approaches. They decided to build the product family around variations in fin angle, number of fin rows, and number of tube columns because these were the easiest parameters to change in manufacturing—yet they provided a performance range sufficient to cover the needs of a wide range of potential customers.

- Explore a very wide range of options for every subsystem, inventing to schedule. By definition, a breakthrough project involves the unknown. Only broad exploration can be certain of finding the breakthrough point. Leave targets loose. Don't decide ahead of time on the technical approach. The only requirement is to get well ahead of the competition, and you can always do that if you let yourself explore broadly. Fall back on conservative solutions for selected parts of the system if you are required to stay on schedule, but consider radical improvements everywhere else.

- Pick conceptually robust solutions that will support a wide variety of tailoring projects for years to come.

• Aim at fully understanding the product family. Ideally, future tailoring projects will only have to read the trade-off curves to design optimized products, generating no new knowledge at all.

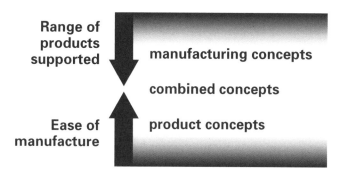

The keys to success in strategic breakthrough projects are:

• Creative and visionary ESD leadership.

• Radical innovation and the resources to support it.

• Keeping up momentum by exploring broadly enough never to get stuck and relentlessly pressing forward.

• Changing the behavior of manufacturing engineers. Manufacturing engineers are used to innovating in support of product innovations. In strategic breakthroughs, they must innovate without waiting for product development.

Re-integration and limited innovation projects innovate in selected subsystems, while re-integrating the system as a whole in order to produce the effect of innovation allowing maximum re-use. They usually target a specific market segment and produce a single product rather than a broad family.

• Most Toyota automobile development projects fit this category. The appearance of the car changes, and some subsystems are innovative, but most elements of the car are merely tailored to the new arrangement. The basic system concept does not change.

- Special machine projects usually are re-integrations with limited innovation. Designers buy every possible component from stock, focusing their creativity on a few selected components or a clever re-arrangement of the entire system.

- High-tech companies often use this strategy because some components are evolving so much faster than others.

Reintegration and limited innovation projects usually are driven by the need for speed and efficiency. The market opportunity is too fleeting and narrow to justify a development effort sufficient to innovate the entire product. (The more complex the product, the more often this is true.) The project must balance achieving enough innovation to satisfy the market and stay competitive, while maximizing re-use to keep costs down.

There are three keys to success in reintegration and limited innovative projects.

- *The subsystem suppliers, external or internal, usually must partially develop innovations prior to and independent of the project.* They will need to tailor the subsystem to the system design, but the more proven it is before the system project starts, the safer. Since the system is being designed mostly from re-used concepts, testing new concepts can throw the entire timing off. For example, Toyota requires suppliers to provide a design show each year in which they show off their new technologies; performance in the design show is a major factor in picking suppliers. Similarly, component designers and manufacturing engineers inside Toyota continuously improve their capabilities. This is a major change in approach for many U.S. companies.

- *The ESDs, and the departmental specialists, must quickly and correctly decide which elements to innovate and which to treat conservatively.* They must be open to new concepts where they offer significant advantages but maintain a conservative bias toward the tried and proven. For example, Toyota must design new stamping dies for every new car in order to meet the market's requirements for new styling. But the fixture points that support the car body during welding are common across car lines and decades. So, too, is the number of die hits used for each body part and the work done by each die. There is in essence a common process for shaping each part even though the shapes are different from car to car.

- *The team must be familiar with the available subsystem solutions and clever in seeing opportunities for new system integrations.* The brilliant products of Lockheed's skunkworks were mostly limited innovations, with parts of existing airplanes recombined to achieve completely new system capabilities.

- *The team must focus on understanding the trade-offs.* Good trade-off knowledge is essential in tuning the design and deciding where to innovate.

Research and demonstration projects aim at producing knowledge, not a product. Trade-off curves are their only output. They may build and field test prototypes but only to gather knowledge. They can therefore focus on a single concept. They don't need redundancy to assure success because success is not required. Indeed, they should normally try to isolate the key aspect of the new concept and gather data about that aspect while faking the rest of the system.

Research projects were heavily used in the American aircraft industry between World War I and World War II because of lack of money to build systems. For example, the NACA (National Advisory Committee for the Commission for Aeronautics, 1915–1958, and then became NASA) used wind tunnel tests to produce extensive catalogs of airfoil performance. Once the money was available, this data enabled fast airplane development.

Sometimes a demonstration project produces something that is immediately useful. If so, fine; reinforce the team as required and make it work. Just don't hand it to someone else, and tell that someone else to make it work.

Research project keys to success are:

- *Speed.* Because research projects don't have an external customer, they tend to slow down. The company needs to demand a constant and rapid flow of new knowledge from the research organization.

- *Trade-off curve focus.* Conventional research projects often just try something new. Unless the research produces a clear understanding of performance limits, it cannot guide future development.

- *Gather as much knowledge as possible from outside the company.*

- *Don't allow Research or Advanced Development to select a concept for product development.* Product Development makes any use it can of the data and ideas created by Research, but it always starts with complete freedom to do whatever makes sense. Research or advanced development concepts are unproven because they have not been produced in volume or used by customers. Development teams must search many concepts to be confident of success.

Conventional companies often use advanced development to make the fundamental, conceptual decisions about products, creating a disastrous hand-off between advanced development and product development. They often attempt limited innovation without requiring component groups to get ahead of system development—and find the system design held up while the component concept is tested. And they cannot run projects to predictable cycles.

Careful classification of projects, and rigorous discipline in sticking to the classification, will dramatically reduce the chaos and improve resource availability and return on investment.

DO
Implement project types

- Clearly define each project type. Identify some examples of projects that got in trouble by confusing types, estimate the cost to the company, and publicize.

- Decide which kinds of project are appropriate for your company. Some companies use re-integration and limited-innovation projects almost exclusively because their systems are too complex, and innovation is too slow for strategic-breakthrough projects. Others focus on strategic-breakthrough and tailoring projects. Most companies need a small, efficient research operation generating new ideas and new trade-off curves.

- You may have an advanced development operation that produces what it imagines are "products." Reclassify such projects as either research and demonstration projects or strategic-development projects. If the project is a strategic-development project, reinforce the team as required and keep it together all the way through launch.

- Define a standard "cycle time" for each kind of project and stick to it.

- Look hard at existing projects while you manage the transition. You probably have a hodge-podge of more or less limited-innovation projects operating to a wide variety of schedules, any of them attempting too much innovation for too small a market. Be ruthless if a project is going to fail. The sooner you kill it, the better. Don't start any new projects until they've been clearly classified.

Why and when to explore broadly

Now we turn to the fundamental question—how broadly should you explore to achieve maximum profit?

Begin your SBCE development by breaking the product down into subsystems, and generating multiple alternatives for each subsystem as well as alternative system arrangements. Some subsystem concepts may work in many system alternatives; in other cases, choosing a different system design will result in totally different subsystems, for instance the way sail and power boats are dissimilar in design. However, the fundamental physics and customer needs may still be similar, so the knowledge you gather may be useful for both system concepts, even though the designs are very different.

Lean developers pursue different numbers of alternatives for different subsystems. For example, a new Toyota is likely to involve 10 to 20 exhaust system prototypes, four to five transmission designs (simulated but not prototyped), and three air-conditioning prototypes. Yet in many cases, the engine and basic manufacturing process are decided before development even begins.

How many alternatives should you explore for each subsystem? Looking at multiple alternatives isn't free, though it is more economical than you might think because teams learn to do it efficiently. Lean developers converge on a single solution at very different times for different subsystems. And of course, convergence has many meanings. We may be talking about fundamentally different system concepts or minor variations in part dimensions.

We should not converge while:

- There is no proven solution or possibly there are much better alternatives to the proven solution, so the team needs redundancy to ensure success. For example, in Denso's strategic development projects, every subsystem designer must consider a very wide range of solutions in order to be sure of finding a good one in so novel a system concept. This is the most common consideration; we use SBCE primarily to make every project successful.

- The team needs to develop trade-off curves or other comparative data in order to optimize the system. This is the basic insight behind *Taguchi methods* or *robust engineering*, which are special cases of SBCE. Consider again the NACA airfoil catalogs; until we systematically explore the space of possibilities, how do we know which is better for a given situation? Sango typically builds 10 to 20 exhaust systems for each Toyota because the right sound can be found only by testing. (Toyota products may sound quieter than competing cars that show lower decibels on electronic noise measurements.) Optimizing by considering multiple subsystem alternatives in parallel is usually much cheaper than optimizing by sequentially developing complete systems.

- The data to make a decision isn't available yet. For example, Toyota holds open the design of sheet metal parts at the front of the car long after the rear parts have been frozen because the front of the car must be optimized for crashworthiness—a slow process.

- Potential problems with more critical subsystems require this subsystem to remain flexible. For example, cooling fan designers are required to be prepared to fit the fan into a variety of possible spaces until quite late in the development process. This allows for the possibility of packaging problems with the power-train, suspension, and styling, all of which converge before the cooling fan. Late convergence in the cooling fan is acceptable because tooling can be constructed quickly and because cooling fans will work across a wide range of sizes. The small ones just make more noise.

Looking the other way, we must converge in time to finish the project. So what can we do?

- Gather data fast.

- Look for conceptually robust solutions.

- Explore just broadly enough to maintain a high probability of success—say, above 95%.

Why do we need such a high probability of success? Because unsuccessful projects not only are expensive, they disrupt the whole company, throwing the schedule of the project off. Frequent failures also make it impossible to appropriately evaluate and learn from developer performance.

Unfortunately, our intuitions generally are wrong about how many options to keep open. We instinctively narrow too quickly. This includes me. My worst mistakes as owner and chief engineer of a special machine company have come from not taking my own SBCE advice.

Developers naturally are quick to make the key system decisions—the ones that drive the rest of the design—so that they can get on with subsystem design. For example, the space shuttle is designed around the decision to make it land like an airplane; a vertical launch and parachute recovery system would have required very different subsystems. However, this decision should have been held open longer, until enough subsystem design had been done to be sure the system concept made sense. The shuttle turned out to be an expensive method of placing pounds in orbit. We often will need to shift our attention up and down the system breakdown, looking at key subsystem alternatives in some detail before making the system decisions.

We can improve our intuitions about how many alternatives to pursue at any point in the process by applying a little basic probability. Here's an easy example, a bicycle design.

Imagine a conventional company with four bicycle-design projects. Each bicycle has five subsystems: frames, gears, brakes, suspension, and wheels.

The conventional company will conceive of a system design for each project, then subsystem designs that best support the system design. Let's imagine the company is trying to be innovative, so its accepts some risk in these designs. Specifically, there is a 20% chance that each subsystem will cause major problems (market miss, project delay, etc.), and a 40% chance that the subsystems won't work well together.

We'll use three rules of probability:

1) The probability of failure is one minus the probability of success (and vice versa).

2) The probability of a number of independent events happening at the same time is the product of the individual probabilities.

3) The average number of occurrences of an event in a series of trials is the probability of occurrence in each trial, times the number of trials.

In the following table, Rule 1 gives the probabilities of success for each subsystem. Then, since all the subsystems have to work for the bicycle to work, Rule 2 gives the total probability of success by multiplying the subsystem probabilities (including the probability of the subsystems working together).

Subsystem	Prob. of Success
Frames	0.8
Gears	0.8
Brakes	0.8
Suspension	0.8
Wheels	0.8
System integration	0.6
Total	0.20

The total probability of success is a disastrously low 20%! Actually, this is probably close to the average fraction of completely successful projects—projects that hit the market on time, in budget, and without quality issues.

Rule 1 now says that the probability of failure for each project is 0.80. By Rule 2, the probability that all four projects will fail is the product of the individual probabilities of failure, or $(0.8)^4 = 0.41$. Or, for every four projects the company does, they have a 0.59 probability that at least one project will succeed, by Rule 1.

Now, imagine a lean company and its suppliers designing bicycles. The lean suppliers would design multiple interchangeable component concepts. Assuming still four concepts per component with a 20% probability of failure, the probability of failure of all the options for a given component is only $(0.2)4 = 0.0016$ by Rule 2. On average, we will get $4(0.8) = 3.2$ successful designs for each component (Rule 3). Of course, all the components have to succeed for the project to succeed. The probability that all the components will have at least one successful alternative is $(1-0.0016)5 = 0.992$ (Rules 1 and 2 again).

We can improve these odds even further by retaining the old and proven solution as part of the set. Then, the project can fail only if all the new concepts fail—a probability so low we can safely ignore it completely.

Still, the components also have to work together. Let's suppose that because the components have been designed more independently than before, there is only a 12% probability that a given set of functioning components will work together—a factor of

5 reduction from the 60% chance we had before. On average, there will be 3.25=336 possible combinations of successful component designs. So, by Rules 1 and 2, the probability that none of them works is $(1-0.12)336=2.35 \times 10^{-19}$. We can safely ignore this number—if we had been running one project per second since the universe began, we would almost certainly have never had a failure.

Further, if we try all the possible combinations, Rule 3 says we statistically can expect $(0.12)(336)=40$ good designs, versus 0.8 for the conventional approach![17]

The risk calculation now looks like this:

Projects				Probability	Number of products	Expected # of products
A	B	C	D			
0.2	0.2	0.2	0.2	0.0016	4	0.0064
0.2	0.2	0.2	0.8	0.0064	3	0.0192
0.2	0.2	0.8	0.2	0.0064	3	0.0192
0.2	0.2	0.8	0.8	0.0256	2	0.0512
0.2	0.8	0.2	0.2	0.0064	3	0.0192
0.2	0.8	0.2	0.8	0.0256	2	0.0512
0.2	0.8	0.8	0.2	0.0256	2	0.0512
0.2	0.8	0.8	0.8	0.1024	1	0.1024
0.8	0.2	0.2	0.2	0.0064	3	0.0192
0.8	0.2	0.2	0.8	0.0256	2	0.0512
0.8	0.2	0.8	0.2	0.0256	2	0.0512
0.8	0.2	0.8	0.8	0.1024	1	0.1024
0.8	0.8	0.2	0.2	0.0256	2	0.0512
0.8	0.8	0.2	0.8	0.1024	1	0.1024
0.8	0.8	0.8	0.2	0.1024	1	0.1024
0.8	0.8	0.8	0.8	0.4096	0	0
					Sum	0.8000

The lean company has a risk—a probability of total failure—of 1% versus 41% for the conventional company. Lean development—SBCE—is much more reliable than conventional development.

17. To calculate the expected number of products resulting from the conventional approach, multiply the probability of each of the 16 possible combinations of successful/failed projects by the number of successful projects for that combination (Rule 2), and sum (Rule 3). I.e., P(Proj A succeeds)*P(Proj B fails)*P(Proj C fails)*P(Proj D fails)*(1 product) + P(Proj A succeeds)*P(Proj B succeeds)* P(Proj C fails)* P(Proj D fails)*(2 products) + ... = (0.2)(0.8)(0.8)(0.8)(1) + (0.2)(0.2)(0.8)(0.8)(2) + ... = 0.8.

FYI: Do the math

Don't like my assumptions? Try out your own. Use calculations like these to determine how many alternatives to carry forward, at the system level or for any subsystem. Continually ask yourself:

"What is the probability of failure for each of the ideas I am now considering for my subsystem?"

"What is the overall probability of failure for my subsystem—the product of the probabilities for the individual concepts?"

"What is the expected cost of failure—the cost to the whole system if I fail—times the probability of failure?"

"What can I cheaply do to reduce the probability of failure—say, add an alternative, run a test, create a trade-off curve?"

"What effect will this step have on the probability of failure?"

"Is it worth it?"

"Okay," I hope you're saying, *"I believe that SBCE is more reliable than conventional design. But it also is a lot more expensive—we had to look at 336 combinations of possible designs!"*

Well, let's look at cost. I hope you'll agree that the best measurement is *cost per successful design*. The lean developers haven't spent the same amount of money on component design, developing the same number of components, so we need only to worry about the cost of looking at combinations of components.

However, we can't look only at the component costs; we also have to consider the system-integration costs. Let's imagine that for the conventional company, development of one bicycle costs $1 million; of this, 30%, or $300,000, is system-integration costs. Then, the conventional company doing four projects will spend 4($700,000) = $2.8 million on component development, and 4($300,000) = $1.2 million on integration, for a total of $4 million divided by 0.8 = $5 million per successful design. The lean companies will spend the same $2.8 million on component development. They will be looking at a lot of alternative systems (336)—most of them in not much detail because some other system clearly will be superior—so let's assume it costs them only 1/5 as much on average to look at a system alternative. Then, they'll spend (336)($300,000)/5 = $20 million on system integration. Since they get 40 successful products out of this, the cost per successful product is ($20,000,000+$2,800,000)/40 = $574,000—about 1/9 the cost per successful product as the conventional company.

What if you wanted only one product? On average, you'd have to try 1/(0.12) = 8.3 combinations of components, for a cost of $2.8 million in component development and (8.3)($60,000) in system integration costs, or a total of $3.3 million. Likely, you wouldn't be this good at integration—but on the other hand, you could develop fewer subsystem alternatives and still have a very high probability of success. However, you can see why lean companies tend to prefer to develop families of designs simultaneously (using strategic breakthrough projects); it drastically reduces the cost per successful design.

FYI: Real-world experience

Don't like my numbers? The interesting thing is that real-world experience suggests something like these economics, though the participants seem to have learned them the hard way rather than calculating them.

There used to be bicycle companies that designed complete bicycles from the top down. These are now gone, replaced by companies that design and build the subsystems, and companies that integrate the systems. In fact, you can easily design your own system, going to a bicycle shop and ordering the components you want to put together. The story is the same in small computers. Standardized interfaces and an SBCE approach has replaced total system companies with subsystem suppliers and system integrators.

"Aha," you say. "Bicycles and computers are special cases. Computer interfaces are simple because interface function is nearly independent of interface geometry. Bicycle interfaces are simple because bicycles are physically 'strung out' so the interactions and geometric constraints are weak. So it's easy to design bicycle and computer components to be interchangeable. But interchangeability is nearly impossible for almost every other product, including mine."

Absolutely right. But lean companies achieve the same benefits, even for highly integrated systems, by learning the following skills:

- Use *conceptual* robustness so that your *concepts* (not the actual parts) are interchangeable;

- *Negotiate at the interfaces* to optimize the system while developing trade-off curves for the parts;

- Focus on *building trade-off knowledge* so that the final tailoring of actual parts that do fit is easy.

To summarize: You can calculate for yourself the probability of a successful design, and the cost per successful design. SBCE can improve both measures dramatically—if you can evaluate systems faster and cheaper than you do now. That is the subject of the next section.

Simple models, independent innovation, aggressive elimination

SBCE demands aggressive evaluation. Conventional development selects a concept for the system, then supporting concepts for subsystems, and then tests to prove that they work. Lean SBCE generates many concepts in parallel, and tries to quickly and efficiently make them fail. It converges on a concept only after proof that it is the best of the set, that it works well with the rest of the system, and that its failure points lie safely beyond operating conditions. Every SBCE team I've advised found their final concept seemed inferior at the start.

The result is lower over-all cost, provided that alternatives can be cheaply evaluated early in the development process. If the cheapest way to evaluate a concept is to manufacture and sell it, you should work on one concept at a time. But usually the cost of evaluating a concept rises rapidly as the project moves toward launch. Thus, as shown below, SCBE "front-loads" the process, evaluates alternatives early and cheaply, and finishes sooner and more certainly, reducing total resource consumption (the area under the green curves).

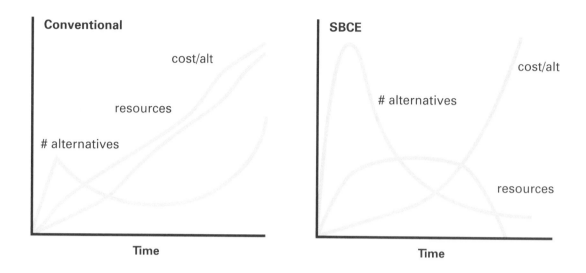

So how do you do it? How do you aggressively evaluate and eliminate concepts?

There are two good reasons to eliminate a concept:

1) *There are enough more profitable, better-tested concepts* to assure success through redundancy. Even at the beginning you can kill a concept by showing that it can't be as good as the existing, market-proven design. Do this using the decision matrices we discussed in the section on ESDs (See Page 85). Later, risk calculations, like those of the last section, will show that you don't need a concept to be reasonably sure of success; other concepts have been tested out far enough.

2) *The concept is fatally flawed.* And how do you cheaply show that a concept is fatally flawed? If possible, develop trade-off curves to show that no such concept can possibly work. For example, it violates the first law of thermodynamics. (More on trade-off curves soon.) Otherwise, figure out what could go wrong—the weak links in the design—and attack those weak links sneakily, cheaply, quickly. Build a "red team" evaluation organization that gets good at this.

Make a list of the things that could go wrong and test first those most likely to defeat the concept. There is no point in testing against threats that aren't dangerous! If you have FMEAs (Failure Modes and Effects Analysis), you can use them. Otherwise, just make a list of failure modes, and start using them to try to kill the concept. As you develop trade-off curve sheets, they will become your primary record of failure modes.

You can kill concepts using analysis, simulations, or prototypes—whatever is cheapest. For example, Sango normally prototypes exhaust systems—10 to 20 per Toyota—because sound quality is difficult to model and exhaust systems are cheap to prototype. Similarly, Denso normally prototypes air conditioning systems before designing them—it is cheaper to have a skilled technician throw together a prototype than to have an engineer detail the design.

Conversely, Aisin AI normally simulates four or five transmissions, but builds only one expensive prototype. And don't forget "back-of-the-envelope" calculations; they often are the fastest and most informative evaluation tool.

Don't rely too much on your list of failure modes, though. The most dangerous failure mode is the one you haven't thought of yet. So get out into the field with some kind of prototype as quickly and cheaply as you can, to help you find the failure modes. Be creative. Even the crudest prototype can help you to find potential problems.

Here are some powerful and simple "prototyping" techniques:

- Walk through the processes of building and using the product, using large paper pads and sticky notes.
- Modify an existing design—yours or a competitor's—to exhibit some of the characteristics of the new design. (In particular, you can sometimes "cripple" a more capable design to see how a cheaper design would work in the field.)
- Build mock-ups of products and manufacturing systems out of foam.

The most common failure mode probably is failure to fit together, so find ways to integrate as much of the system as possible, as soon as possible. Toyota builds many more early "integration prototypes" than do conventional companies, trying to make sure that all the subsystems work together. Use mock-ups made out of foam, foam core, wood, or anything else that's handy. Build partial, low speed manufacturing systems to test tooling concepts. Use virtual assembly computer tools if you have them—but remember that the computer tools don't usually check your manufacturing processes the way a prototype build can.

Find "lead users," who place the greatest demand on the product, need it the most, and are best able to provide intelligent feedback. Taxi drivers in Tunisia, for example, stress a car more in a week than other drivers in a year. Don't forget to use the product yourself. Scientific instruments and rock-climbing equipment usually are designed by users. Establish intellectual property agreements and bring the user fully into the development process—they will find failure modes you miss.

Finally, train and organize aggressive and independent evaluators—"red teams." Test and simulation experts are supposed to make concepts fail, then tell you why they failed and what to do about it. Don't let them perform standard tests only. For example, a U.S. door-control module went through a set of standard tests that took three weeks and found 15 bugs. The Japanese customer then sent one of their test engineers, who "played with the simulator" and found another 30 bugs in three days.

Put simulation experts in the test organization. This makes it easy to decide whether to use simulation or testing to evaluate. More important, testing must check all simulation models. Design engineers should do as much of their own simulation and testing as possible to give them hands-on feel. But you still need an independent test organization. Design engineers want the product or production system to succeed. Testers need to make it fail.

Evaluate in four phases:

1. Quick and dirty tests, simulations, and analytic models to guide innovation and quickly kill the weaker concepts.

2. Quick field tests to find unexpected failure modes.

3. More systematic evaluations to produce trade-off curves to guide optimization and prevent field failures. For example, a family of muffler designs can be characterized by a curve relating back-pressure in the muffler to noise at a given engine output, as we saw on Page 115. Said a Sango engineer: "We have built as many as 10 to 20 exhaust systems for every Toyota project because the chief engineer wants to know what the trade-offs are." Once the chief knows what this curve looks like, he can decide where he wants his car to operate. And the data are useful for future projects as well as this one.

4. Operational stress tests to check the accuracy of earlier simulations and find unanticipated problems. Here, we are testing the whole system.

But you can't ever test enough to make sure the product works. Six Sigma quality implies that no reasonable amount of testing will uncover most field failures. (Showing conformance to specification, where needed, can normally be arranged as a side effect of testing to failure.) You have to test to failure, so as to improve your trade-off curves. Then, the trade-off curves (not the tests) guide the design. This is the subject of the next section.

Trade-off curves

How can you turn data into useable knowledge? How can you design to have almost no field failures? How can you stop the waste of discarding knowledge? How can you guide the design toward optimality? How can you ensure that suppliers are being honest? How can you understand customer needs better than the customers do? How can you make sure your products are manufacturable?

By using *trade-off curves*. If I could teach you only one lean tool, trade-off curves would be the one.

The best example of the use of trade-off curves comes from WWII America. The P-51 Mustang—perhaps the finest piston engine fighter ever built—was designed and put in production in four months. That is a lean development process! In the 1990s Jose Rodriguez, then a consultant for the Parametrics Technology Corp., interviewed some surviving members of the development team. They told him the key was knowing most of the trade-off curves before development began. For example, before the war the National Advisory Committee for Aeronautics (NASA's predecessor) exhaustively cataloged airfoils, recording lift and drag as functions of Reynolds number and angle of attack.

But, the developers said, after the war the aeronautics industry discovered computers. With computers, one first designed, then simulated, then re-designed, then re-simulated, etc. The art of capturing trade-off curves was lost. The time required to bring a fighter airplane into production grew to 20 years.

Trade-off curve sheets were the only element of the lean development system that Toyota people seemed reluctant to discuss. Trade-off curve sheets typically are 11-by-17 inches, or European "A3" size (or two standard sheets facing each other). This size enables you to see the whole picture without having to try to remember something you looked at earlier and forces you to boil information down into simple, visual form.

They usually include:

- A picture of the part and/or process.

- A statement of the failure mode being considered.

- An analysis of the cause.

- Possible countermeasures.

- A graph showing the conditions under which the failure mode occurs. See the example.

Part and process: Forged neck tie rods

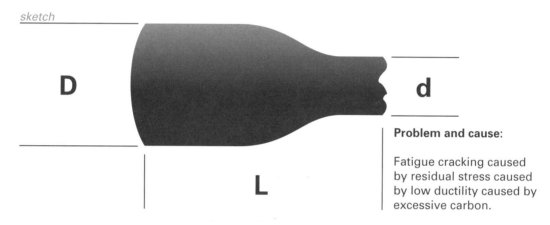

sketch

D

d

L

Problem and cause:

Fatigue cracking caused by residual stress caused by low ductility caused by excessive carbon.

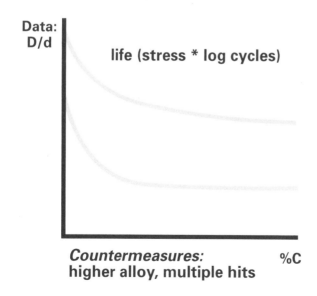

Data: D/d

life (stress * log cycles)

Countermeasures: **higher alloy, multiple hits**

%C

The graph is the key; it shows the limits of what can be done with a particular technology. It represents data in visual form, turning it into usable knowledge. Even if the curve is derived from an equation or simulation, the graph is better because developers can instantly understand and apply it. Toyota design groups then create engineering check sheets that summarize the key points from the trade-off curve studies into a compact and efficient form for use in design reviews.

Simple enough. So how do you develop them, who does the work, and how do you use them?

Start developing trade-off curve sheets in workshops. Later, as people gain experience, they can do them by themselves. Use the people actually doing the work (not a group of trade-off curve specialists or staff experts—though you'll need specialists to teach people how to make the curves). Each departmental group—say, the people who design doors—needs to maintain its own book of trade-off curves, making them available to the rest of the organization.

Begin with parts, CAD models, or big sketches on an easel pad, whiteboard, or transparency. Later, reduce everything to a single, simplified drawing on your A3 paper.

Focus on a single failure mode to begin with. Later, you may be able to combine more data onto a single sheet, but start with just one.

You can approach the cause and countermeasure analysis as a graph. Write the failure mode in red on the left side of a white board. Write the immediate causes in red to the right, with connecting arrows. Keep tracing back through the causes. Write countermeasures in green, showing where they interrupt the chain of failure.

Plot the key data showing when the failure mode occurs—and when it doesn't.

Simplify, simplify, simplify.

Look for the right combination of parameters.

- Good combinations represent a lot of data clearly. For example, the classic airfoil curves plot lift versus drag coefficients, at various Reynolds numbers and angles of attack. Reynolds number is a combination of four parameters (density, viscosity, speed, and some characteristic size). Lift and drag coefficients involve speed, density, force, and area.

- Good combinations clearly show the limits of performance, so you can stay safely inside them.

- Good combinations clarify what to do to improve the situation.

Finding better combinations is an art; plan on improving your trade-off curve sheets forever.

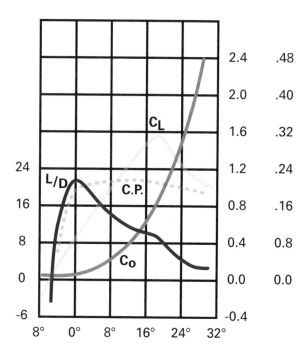

So how do you use trade-off curve sheets?

- As your primary guides to good design. When developing, first build the trade-off sheets; getting the details of the design will then be easy.

- To understand, train, and help remember; not as design rules. (If someone can find a way around the limits stated in a trade-off sheet, great!)

- To evaluate suppliers and their promises; to aid in negotiations.

- To get 6 Sigma quality, with field failure rates below one part in a million. You can't test to that level of quality; you have to design it in, and only trade-off curves can tell you how.

- To sell.

Denso used these skills to take an entire business line away from a customer of mine. Denso first showed the OEM test results demonstrating that the product outperformed my client's products, in the OEM's application. Then, in a pilot buy they delivered a million parts without a defect.

Trade-off curve sheets reflect a basic way of thinking. Most naive engineers approach problems by looking for a solution. When they get an idea that seems plausible, they try it out. When it fails, they try to improve it, again using the first idea that comes to mind. Using this approach, one can debug forever. There is no guarantee that the solution actually will work, and no guarantee that the proposed improvements actually make things better.

Lean engineers always ask first, *"What are the fundamental trade-offs governing the performance of such systems?"* This tells them how to solve the problem and improve performance, and it tells them whether the solution is worth working on. Toyota engineers seem almost unable to talk without sketching some sort of trade-off curve; that is just the way they think.

Implement trade-off curves

Start holding workshops. Revisit, revisit, revisit. Demand to see trade-off curve sheets at all design reviews. Demand them from suppliers and component design groups. Take them to every meeting. Update them at every experiment. Refer to them for every design decision. Incorporate their way of thinking into everything; whenever brainstorming, debugging, or making decisions, ask: *"What's the governing trade-off?"*

I promised you that we'd see how to achieve highly integrated system designs while looking at multiple subsystem alternatives. It's time.

Convergence and negotiation

In bicycles and computers, interfaces are simple and standardized. Therefore, it is easy to produce interchangeable subsystem parts.

Most products are more tightly integrated. Subsystem designs (including manufacturing other parts of the total value stream) affect system designs and vice versa; subsystem designs affect each other. Most subsystem alternatives are not interchangeable. So, how can you apply a set-based approach?

By holding the subsystem designers responsible for negotiating their own interfaces, while managing their own convergence processes. There is one simple rule: Impose constraints on others if and only if you know they are needed. Otherwise, negotiate with the people who have the most knowledge.

For example, a Toyota dashboard designer told me, "One critical problem is the allocation of space between the air handling unit and the stereo system. I tell the suppliers of each of these, 'I may give you 4 centimeters of height, or I may give you 6 or 8. Tell me what you can do for me with each amount of space.' We make the final decision based on how much each component can contribute to the car with the different amounts of space." The Toyota dashboard designer is able to draw on the most up-to-date knowledge of the stereo and HVAC designers, and they can make a joint decision better than any one of them could alone.

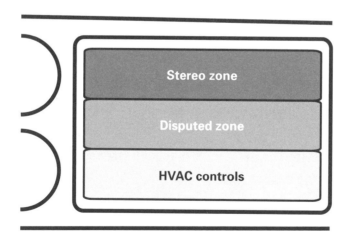

Another example: Toyota sheet metal designs are released without tolerances. Stamping is a black art, so sheet metal parts rarely match drawings when die makers first try out the die. This causes unacceptable appearance problems where the parts meet. The conventional (expensive) solution is to put tight tolerances on the stamped parts, and adjust the die by sanding until the parts are within tolerance.

Toyota gets the best fits in the industry without tolerances and at much lower cost by a process called "functional build." At the beginning of die try out, manufacturing engineers assemble a car from the stamped parts. Of course, the fit isn't good enough. So, the engineers modify the dies in the cheapest possible way to improve the fit, without regard to which parts are furthest from the nominal design.

The functional build process transfers some of the responsibility for achieving good fit from the product engineers (who in a conventional process would assign tolerances), to the manufacturing engineers who design the dies. (The product engineers are still responsible for designing parts that are easy to fit together.) This makes sense, because the manufacturing engineers have the most direct knowledge of the fit issue.

Note, though, that functional build only makes sense because stamping is much more *repeatable* than it is *predictable*. The dies (properly used in a disciplined process) produce parts that are very similar to each other; they just aren't very similar to the drawing. Unless the manufacturing process is repeatable, a functional build process will just chase its tail, changing things back and forth.

Also notice that the dies either have to be made inside Toyota or made by a supplier with which Toyota has an intimate relationship. Tolerances form the basis of a contract: The supplier gets paid when the parts delivered are in tolerance. Without tolerances, the supplier must trust Toyota to be fair about when they pay and who has to make changes.

The "minimum constraint" principle applies to constraints of timing as well. For example, the most difficult timing issue in automobile development is the interaction among body design, crash testing, die design, build, and tryout. The body design can't be finalized without crash test results, which require prototypes. Dies can't be built without a body design. And there isn't time to do a preliminary body design, build prototypes, get crash results, finalize the body design, and design, build, and try out the dies in sequence. Die build and tryout alone takes 72 weeks at most U.S. companies.

Conventional companies order the dies before finishing crash tests, and pay for changes later. Die builders say that they would go broke building dies at the price they bid them. They make money only on changes.

The Toyota solution is to negotiate gradual convergence on the final solution, making decisions as soon as there is enough data. That is, Toyota engineers freeze and release the designs of the rear of the car first, because crash issues don't affect the rear. This "rolling release" moves forward and inward, so that the last parts to be released for die design are the front inner members, because these dies are relatively simple and fast to build and tryout. Toyota reserves space in die shops for these last components, pre-orders materials, and even has standard features cut on the dies while waiting for the decisions on the final surfaces. Even after die manufacture, Toyota still can make final adjustments by changing sheet metal thickness on inner parts. This requires at most some minor resanding of the die surface.

Changing sheet metal thickness at the last minute can compensate for problems with the shape of parts, which must be frozen much sooner. This suggests a corollary to the principle:

Maintain enough flexibility in the design of some short-lead-time subsystems to compensate for problems with long-lead-time items.

Radiator fan design is an example. One radiator fan designer (for a Toyota supplier) told me that on a project with two major prototype builds, he would only know his size targets to within about 30% at the first build, and 5% at the second. He would have prototypes in different sizes to allow for this uncertainty.

Toyota was exploiting both the short lead times for fan design, prototyping, and manufacturing equipment build and the fact that fans of various sizes will all work if they fit in the space; smaller fans are just noisier and less efficient. So, Toyota could use a last-minute choice of fans to compensate for packaging problems with the styling; engine, and suspension—items where space and performance effects were more critical, and lead times longer.

Got the idea? Letting the interfaces "breathe"—negotiating how things fit together—lets you explore multiple alternatives even for highly integrated systems, and arrive at a well-optimized design. Negotiating the convergence process—"*I need you to make a final decision by Oct. 15th.*"—allows you to optimize the development process.

Implement negotiated targets and interfaces

This is going to be a tough one. All of your engineers have been taught that the way to get a good product is to tightly constrain it, with tight specifications and tolerances. You may have spent a lot of money on tolerance stack-up software and training in geometric dimensioning and tolerancing. And your organization probably hasn't built up much trust from suppliers and between product and manufacturing engineers.

So, pick your targets carefully. Brief all the people who might get upset; give them a chance to argue. Quietly pull together small teams of the people who actually are doing the work, give them the ideas, and help them figure out how to do it. If they refuse, try somewhere else.

Monitor the results, both to make sure that people stick to the new concepts, and to make sure nothing disastrous happens.

So much for SBCE. It's a powerful tool for reducing risk and increasing innovation. But it ties conventional project management schemes—task-based methodologies such as the critical path or critical chain methods—in knots. There are too many options; the plan has to be adjusted too much as we go. So, lean companies need a simpler, more flexible project management system. And that is the subject of the next section.

Cadence, flow, pull

Any development, but especially an SBCE development, is complex and constantly changing. New problems and opportunities emerge as the team learns. One U.S. team leader put it this way: "This is like surfing. You constantly adjust, changing direction, shifting from wave to wave."

In such a highly variable environment, how can:

- *Developers know what to do, when?*

- *The right information get to the right place at the right time?*

- *Managers be confident that projects will be finished, on time, with good results?*

Conventional project management attempts to answer these questions by defining a detailed plan and trying to stick to it. Instead of learning to surf, conventional organizations try to control the waves! This almost never works.

Toyota has taken most of a century to learn how to surf—how to operate smoothly yet flexibly. Toyota project management (like Toyota plant operations) rests on four concepts: *cadence*, *flow*, *pull*, and *value-creating management*.

Cadence means that everything moves to a repetitive rhythm, like a heartbeat. Cadence lets us drain the chaos from development, level the load on resources, and continuously and rapidly improve operations.

Flow means that knowledge and material are available when needed, in bite-sized chunks that can be handled easily.

Pull means that everyone responds directly to the needs of their customers, producing as required.

Value-creating management means that supervisors directly create value, designing systems and adding and spreading knowledge.

These concepts intertwine throughout this section. You'll apply them as you learn how to:

- Use target events—hands-on design reviews—to pull the development team forward and assure success.

- Establish an information field from which people can pull as required.

- Establish a cadence of projects.

- Establish rhythmic cycles for all development activities, so that everything moves forward steadily, and knowledge is generated in a smooth flow.

- Establish a rhythmic cadence for individuals, so that people know when they can get knowledge from each other, and they can work with minimum interruptions.

- Convert managers from giving directives and demanding reports to effectively supporting the frontline developers.

Before we get to these skills, however, let's look in more detail at what's wrong with conventional project management—and with many efforts to apply lean manufacturing thinking to development.

What's the problem with conventional project management?

Is there a problem? *"After all,"* many development managers say, *"every time we have a problem, we find that we weren't following our process. If we could just discipline our people to follow the process, we would eliminate the problems."*

But we know something's seriously wrong with conventional project management because the companies that work hardest at it—defense companies—have the slowest and most expensive development processes. And there is a direct experiment. In the 1980s, Ford and GM began emphasizing project management, developing detailed, standardized schedules and trying to discipline the company to follow them. Chrysler, drawing on observations of Honda, instead drastically simplified and loosened its process. Chrysler's efficiency and profitability promptly soared far beyond Ford and GM.[18]

Innumerable skunkworks and co-located cross-functional teams have rediscovered the same lessons. Conventional development process concepts lead to tremendous waste; getting rid of process in favor of teamwork and enthusiasm produces immediate, dramatic improvements.

So why not just do that? Why do we need to worry about development process management at all? Because in large companies, the informal methods only work for a little while. Soon, they lead to spectacular failures, and the pendulum swings back. Skunkworks are replaced by bureaucracy. Chrysler is even now exploring establishing a more formal process.

Why? Because informal processes in large companies work because people remember how to do things based on the previous formal process—and they work only as long as people remember.

Teams excused from conventional controls work hard because they are finally being given freedom. They cut corners, "do what makes sense," eliminate waste, and do great things. But as time goes on, the system wanders further and further into idiosyncrasy and confusion. Institutional memory disappears. No one knows what they are supposed to do, or when. A major failure occurs, and the company tries to build a controlling schedule again. It keeps adding controls until everything slows down so far that the formal system has to be junked again.

So conventional thinking traps us in a vicious cycle. We can make things better for a while by abandoning process in favor of enthusiasm. But sooner or later we have to

18. This was the author's understanding at the time of writing.

put them back. To break this cycle of stifling over-control and scary under-control—both leading to chaos and sluggish development—we need to understand why conventional process thinking creates waste.

Conventional thinking—scientific management applied to development—says that:

- People should be told what to do, in as much detail as possible.

- Detailed schedules are required so that things are done in the right sequence.

- Knowledge should flow through channels, as precisely defined as possible.

This thinking pervades the conventional tools for planning and managing projects. (If you aren't familiar with these tools, good; you haven't learned bad habits, and I'll tell you all you need to know anyway.) Critical path, PERT, critical chain methods, process engineering charts, and process flow charts all use the same two basic concepts:[19]

1. "Task" boxes tell people what to do.

2. Arrows that connect them, representing either dependency (Do Task 1 before Task 2.) or information channels (Task 1 supplies information to Task 2), or both.

19. Later in his thinking, but not yet reflected in his writings at the time of his death, Al Ward began moving away from his highly critical view of some of these tools and methods for understanding and (re)designing processes. First, many sub-processes within product development are repetitive, such as processing purchase orders, and should be optimized in terms of waste, standardized, and continuously improved—some of the tools listed are ideally suited for these tasks, and Al became a strong believer in the use of tools for this purpose. Second, in practice he found that some of the tools, in particular value stream mapping adapted for product development, could be extremely useful in generating a common understanding of developer knowledge and work flow, in making wastes and bottlenecks visible, and in pointing the way toward focused process improvement efforts. The problems noted later are not problems with the tools per se, but how they are used. For example, "task boxes tell people what to do" is true if one department draws the box-and-arrow diagram, and another is expected to execute against it. However, if the diagram is used as a way for a development team to get their hands around their own internal processes, or if an individual developer uses one to plan out his work, then this is not the case at all.

All these methods have the following problems.

- *Task boxes tell people what to do. This creates **hand-off** waste.* The people doing the work know the most about what knowledge is needed next and how to get it. Task boxes relieve them of the responsibility for using that knowledge.

- *Arrows create more **hand-off**, showing a transfer of responsibility* from one person to another. (We'll learn how to keep projects on time without transfers of responsibility.)

- *Conventional plans define detailed schedules that produce waste of **scatter**.* The schedule breaks down before the ink is dry, and the team starts expediting.

- *Conventional plans define project length based on adding up the time required for each task on the "critical path."* But **estimates of task length are notoriously unreliable** because there is an enormous variation in circumstances for the tasks. It is far more reliable to classify projects according to type and plan on the same time for every project in the class.

- *Arrows create sequence and, therefore, the waste of **waiting**.* In critical path, PERT, and critical chain methodologies, arrows mean "*X must be done before starting Y*"—for example, design before testing. But in development, a little knowledge now is better than a lot of knowledge later. Waiting to test means that we may spend a lot of effort designing the wrong thing.

- *Arrows create information channels that push rather than pull information, creating **scatter**.* Channels were unavoidable when typewriter and carbon paper reproduced information. But channels create multiple copies of the same information, which get out of date and out of sync with each other. They bombard people with information that they don't need at the time. They create expediting—hours of voice mail—as people try to get the information they need at the moment.

- *Task boxes standardize what people do, thus creating **poor tool waste**.* Most tasks check against already known failure modes—and miss the unexpected failures.

- *Finally, box-and-arrow charts are hopelessly inadequate for set-based concurrent engineering.* SBCE teams decide day to day how to attack which alternatives. Targets and alternatives narrow slowly. Communication runs in all directions. Trying to represent this conventionally can result in an impossibly confusing profusion of boxes and arrows.

So conventional project management won't work. What do we do?

Build a good target event

How can developers coordinate their efforts? How can management be sure the team is making progress?

1) Define a small (three to 10) number of target events, at which the knowledge (or ignorance) of the team will be easy to see.

2) Have all team members make their own plans for achieving those target events.

3) Crosscheck those plans against each other, negotiating any problems developer to developer.

4) Rigorously enforce the target event timing and quality.

(If this seems too simple, remember that Toyota has the best on-time-launch record in the industry.)

Good target events make the team's knowledge or ignorance easy to see because they:

- Answer these key questions:
  - *Do we have a good plan for development?*
  - *Do we understand the possible alternatives?*
  - *Does our product work in the field?*
  - *Can we manufacture it?*

- *Integrate the efforts of the whole team.* Once you put everything the team does together, most problems are highly visible. Plus, you want the target events to pull everyone.

- *Review physical objects backed by trade-off curves.* (When I first taught the senior mechanical design project course at the University of Michigan, we used to spend hours trying to read thick project reports. When I demanded that the students actually build the projects, five minutes watching the machine work and asking questions became enough to assign the grade.)

- *Involve technical experts and senior managers, hands-on.*

During these events, make sure that you are:

- *Doing design reviews where the hardware is—test sites, labs, factories.* Cut the briefings; each reviewer has different interests and expertise. Instead, spread the trade-off curve sheets and the parts on tables, with a development team expert by each. Let reviewers walk around asking questions.

- *Including senior managers as reviewers.* This is their best opportunity to improve future profits. Pair them with outside technical experts. (Preliminary "peer" reviews are a good idea but not a substitute for a hard technical look by "them as can hurt you or help you." Target events have to be important to the developers, or they won't get ready.)

- *Focusing on creating knowledge.* Reviewers have either technical knowledge or a broader picture than the team. So conduct a dialog; start to finish; take notes. Brief back what you've learned to the assembled reviewers, to make sure you aren't making things worse from one perspective while improving them in another.

FYI: A Toyota example

Target events in developing a Toyota might include:

- The project leader's concept briefing to the board of directors. Every one on the team has to "sign-on" to the plan, so it integrates effectively. It makes quality visible because it includes the product vision, sketches, the target-event timeline, budget, performance, and new technology targets. The board and team members easily can crosscheck to see whether the plan makes sense.

- Styling approval. This includes manufacturing sign-off and a structural plan for every important aspect of the car. For example, the body structure plan shows the layout and cross-sections of the framing members. So, the reviewers (including available members of the board of directors) can look back and forth between the clay styling model and the body layout to determine whether the project will work.

- Preliminary integration prototype builds. These assemble the car, though fairly crudely, so that developers can see whether their basic decisions work. One vice president of development was famous for crawling through prototypes marking badly designed parts with large Xs.

- Full prototype builds.

- Manufacturing trials.

As a reviewer, comment negatively on anything the team does "just for the review"; be careful not to be seduced by flashy presentation. Focus on the knowledge. Is it there? Is it right? Does the team understand it? Have they talked to the right people, read the right books and reports, conducted the right analysis and tests, thought about enough alternatives? Do they know why they eliminated some alternatives, and do their reasons make sense? Do they seem to have developed as much knowledge as other teams at the same point in the schedule?

If you define good target events, team members will naturally make their own plans to be ready. All developers plan to meet the knowledge and material needs of their customers—project leaders, other developers, plants, and final customers.

Each individual or sub-team plan is just another, more detailed list of target dates and outcomes or high-level objectives. Plans focus mostly on getting ready for the next major target. For example, before styling approval, the styling department sets dates by which to narrow the alternatives down to three to five clay models, and to review these with manufacturing engineering.

Crosscheck these plans against each other, *across*, *around*, and *down*.

- Developers check *across* departments to *pull* the information that they need. For example, a manufacturing engineer may need final drawings for a part by Nov. 10. He must check with the product engineer before hand to be sure the project engineer plans to finish on time.

- Departmental supervisors check *around* the department, looking for unexplained differences between plans that should be similar, and ensuring that the department can support the plan.

- The project leader checks *down*, making sure that individual plans support the overall plan and dovetail with each other.

Thus, everyone plans his own work. Every time I've seen team leaders plan someone else's work, they have made serious mistakes. Staff planning "experts" make worse mistakes—and their plans usually are so detailed that the mistakes are hard to see. Never assess the quality of a plan by the weight of the paper. A plan that is more than one page is much too long to be understood and followed.

Take planning dates seriously. Being late for a target event at Toyota is among the most serious sins a developer can commit because it delays the entire team. Sacrifice performance, weight, or cost by going with a more conservative solution if necessary in order to make the target event on time. Establish a clear policy that developers must report immediately anything that might cause them to miss a date, and give them plenty of help when they do surface problems. Always assume until proven otherwise that developers are doing their best and need help, not criticism.

Missing a timing target is much more damaging than missing a cost, weight, or performance target. If I have 10% of a project, and am overweight or overcost by 10%, I've hurt the project by 1%. If I'm 10% late, I make the whole project 10% late. And this ripples through other projects, creating destructive scatter and missed market opportunities throughout the entire organization.

DO
Implement pull planning

Pull planning is easy and far more effective than whatever you are doing. Change your QS 9000 procedures if necessary. Use your existing box-and-arrow charts as reference material to help people plan their own work. But set your people free to create, now!

Make sure you implement all parts of the system. Define target events that make the knowledge easily visible. Get participation from both technical experts and the managers who control team members' careers—and use their time well. Make everyone plan and crosscheck the plans. Hold people responsible for being on time—including getting help if necessary.

Classify your projects as we discussed under SBCE, and establish a standard length for each type of project. Compare plans against each other, and question differences between them. Initiative is good, so differences may be good—but the more similar plans are, the more people adjust to them and achieve "unconscious competence." At Toyota, I was told that every plan is done "case by case"—but every developer could draw a "typical" plan from memory.

Pull planning gets projects done on time. It provides the opportunity to eliminate most of the tremendous waste of hand-off inherent in task-based systems. But like everything else in the lean system, it demands very different behavior from management; now is a good time to talk about that behavior.

Value-creating, flow-supporting management

Conventional managers tell people what to do, and demand that people report back that it is done. That's their job.

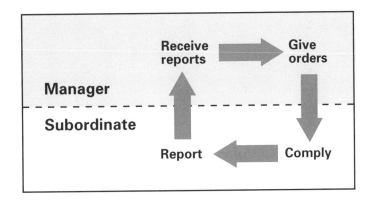

Unfortunately, this means managers take responsibility for what should be done. But the line developer, not the manager, has the most knowledge about what the developer should do. Developers know what they don't know. They have the most feedback from analysis, simulation, testing, and hands-on experience. They know best what they should do.

So conventional management creates the waste of hand-off, separating responsibility from action, knowledge, and feedback. It makes people respond to bureaucratic priorities instead of their development customers, producing the waste of scatter. Managers—presumably the most capable people in the organization when they were promoted—wind up creating waste instead of value. And their own knowledge and ability rapidly decay.

Pull planning changes this, as we've seen. Instead of doing what their bosses tell them to do, developers respond to their customer's needs.

Is this "empowerment" as in "just get the managers out of the way and let people do their jobs?" Some companies have tried this. They often show a spurt of creative brilliance followed by bankruptcy.

Why? Because managers do have a role—a critical one. They understand the big picture better than frontline developers. They must design the way projects fit together. They are (we hope) more experienced or creative than line developers, so they can help developers solve unusual problems. They maintain departmental wisdom, cutting across projects and individual developer's skill. They evaluate developers' work and skills and help developers improve. And they provide rapid reinforcements to help out when teams fall behind.

Let me explain this a little further. Maintaining a smoothly flowing development system requires the ability to quickly add resources at temporary bottlenecks. Otherwise, such routine events as developer vacation or sickness or an unexpectedly difficult test or analysis can disrupt the flow, causing ripples of chaos to spread outward through the system. Most conventional companies expect this and expect late projects.

So, don't overload developers. If you try to do too much, you will do all of it badly. No "process" can change this fact.

The 3M Co. has an ingenious and profitable countermeasure. They authorize developers to spend 15% of their time on projects that the developers themselves initiate. This results in a steady flow of innovations and provides a buffer of time that developers can use if they fall behind on official projects.

However, the 3M solution addresses only minor flow disruptions. You need another way to handle employees leaving the company, getting sick, or falling deeply behind.

Adding a person who is unfamiliar with the project usually slows it down further while they get up to speed. So, lean companies use supervisors as the critical flexible resource. Supervisors are already familiar with each project their sections support. They are experienced developers. They can quickly step in to maintain the momentum and the flow. This critical role of lean supervisors and managers is almost unknown in conventional companies.

So, imagine you are a departmental supervisor, with a section of, say, five mechanical engineers supporting a number of projects developing various kinds of automotive sensors. How do you stay familiar with the projects, guide the developers to improve their knowledge, and make sure things are on track—without disrupting development with orders or demands for reports? How do you add value?

Easily. Replace the conventional waste-making cycle with the fundamental value-creating cycle. Go see; ask why; form good system solutions and inform people of your knowledge.

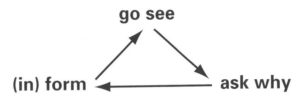

"Go see" means get out of your office and go look at real objects, data, and events. Avoid progress reports; they corrupt data. (Engineers in at least one large aerospace company sometimes "release drawings" with the notation "drawing to be added later," thus "making" the formally required drawing release date.)

Instead:

- Get your hands dirty with lab tests, prototypes, and field trials.

- Go talk to your sections' customers—project leaders, plant personnel, developers who use your people's knowledge, final customers. Review with them the knowledge your section recently provided—data, trade-off curves, drawings. Ask how you can do better. Bring together people who have conflicting views, with their data. That's how to learn. Review data with your people. How well did their designs perform? Why?

- Establish a "no surprises" policy. Hold your people responsible for telling you about potential problems immediately. If you think you need to help out, go where the knowledge is—to the lab or plant, or to meet with other experts.

- Hold daily five-minute stand-up meetings with your section. Ask, *"What are you working on? Where will you be? Are there any big problems?"* Tell them where to reach you.

- Visit each of your people at least once a week. (Visit inexperienced developers daily.) Look at trade-off curves, parts, and CAD and CAE models. Ask questions. If you find a problem, keep asking questions until the developer comes up with a satisfactory set of possible solutions—and a plan for finding which one is right.

- The questions you ask are all variations on "why?" (Remember how your kids drove you crazy with "why?" Made you think, didn't they? That's what you are trying to do—make your people think.)

For example:

- *"Why is the machine doing that?"*

- *"What is the cause of that problem?"*

- *"What alternative solutions did you consider? Why did you choose this one?"*

- *"Who did you talk to about this idea?"*

- *"What are you thinking about doing next? Why? What else have you thought about doing?"*

Be direct. If the explanation you are getting makes you uncomfortable, say, *"I'm feeling uncomfortable. I don't understand why you discarded alternative Y, which makes more sense to me. You said it was because of the difficulty of holding tolerance on this hole, but it seems to me you could redesign like this (make a sketch) so that this tolerance would not be so tight. What am I missing?"*

Teach your subordinates a standard approach to asking you for support or advice. They should always briefly:

- review the background

- state the problem

- analyze the cause

- present the alternative solutions

- recommend the best solution

- state an implementation plan

- state a feedback plan, to assess how well the solution works

Don't try to guide people to the right answer, and don't hide what you think you know. Be completely open with your own knowledge. But don't assume that you are right; always consider the possibility (probability) that you are missing something. Show how you arrived at your answer, and ask for critique.

You'll find that technical expertise helps you but isn't required. Ask your subordinates to teach you, and you'll find that you have taught them. Keep asking "why," and you'll find they do the right thing. You don't have to tell them what to do. (I spent six years in the Army trying to get people to follow orders. Then I became an artificial intelligence programmer. Computers follow orders exactly. What a pain! Give me people who do the right thing, and I won't worry about orders.)

Surface conflict. When you don't understand, say, *"I don't understand. Do you mean X, or Y, or something else?"* When two statements seem to conflict, say, *"You said A. Joe said B. How do these connect?"* Don't be afraid of silence. It lets people think things through. Use silence when people start losing their tempers. Take breaks if needed.

Some people will think your directness and questions are rude—particularly because the questions will reveal their ignorance. Explain your policy. Point out that the universe is infinitely complex, and everyone is ignorant of most things. Ignorance isn't failure; not learning is failure.

Have them read this book. They'll learn. Japan is among the world's most covert societies, yet Toyota has created a remarkably direct culture. Directness is comfortable and efficient.

Others will keep trying to get you to make decisions for them. They'll learn too.

Your "(in)form" action will depend on the results of your questions. Most often, you'll see that someone isn't asking the right question. So, ask them the question, and let them go get the answer. This forms their skills and gets the right question answered.

Sometimes, you have the data they need. Inform them.

Sometimes their data needs to be combined with other data to create usable knowledge. Form a trade-off curve, and inform everyone who needs it. As a manager, you have a much broader picture of the data being gathered in your department than any subordinate does. You can often do a much better job of creating trade-off curves.

Sometimes the development process itself is failing. Form a better development process.

Sometimes there is a conflict between the needs of the project and needs of the company. Form a policy and inform people of it.

Sometimes you'll find a resource shortage. Take on part of the work and form a solution. Start by having the subordinate provide a full briefing on what to do, in the "background, problem, cause, alternatives, recommendation, and implementation" format. You will pursue the root cause of the problem, finding a way to get things back on track. You may gather resources from elsewhere; you may teach the subordinate something; you may actually do the work.

This quick reinforcement role is central to value-creating management:

- It keeps managers technically competent.
- It lets the supervisor see where the problems are.
- It's a powerful motivator for subordinates to stay on schedule. Who really wants their bosses digging deeply into what they've been doing?
- It trains subordinates.
- If the subordinate actually isn't trying, the boss soon will know.
- It keeps everything running smoothly.

Of course, this means that managers need to have time to help! They have to get rid of their old waste-creating responsibilities and focus on adding value.

Project leaders and departmental managers both create value, but they have different responsibilities. Project leaders just try to make the project work, like play-calling quarterbacks. They form and inform as much as they ask. Departmental managers develop people and cross-project knowledge, like coaches. They ask more than they "form"—except when helping out someone who is behind.

Implement value-creating management

Start by implementing pull planning. You can't get managers to stop giving orders if that is the only way to get projects finished. Use every design review as an opportunity to train managers in how to review.

Circulate posters or wallet cards with the value-creating cycle and the six-step problem-solving approach (background, problem, alternatives, recommendation, implementation, feedback).

Hold role-playing workshops to train managers. Have the "subordinate" lay traps for the managers, for example by asking for advice rather than following the six-step problem-solving process.

Use project leaders to informally evaluate departmental managers. Are they adding trade-off curves? Are they teaching? Are they helping people when they fall behind?

Now we turn to one of the most important roles of senior managers: forming the development process itself so as to produce steady rhythm and level resource loads.

Establishing a project cadence

Conventional development organizations are chaotic. Some people work too hard; others don't have enough to do. People miss deadlines, call emergency meetings, and spend hours trying to find each other. Projects start at random intervals and last for random time periods.

Conventional project management techniques promise to reduce the chaos through planning. This promise is false. Conventional management creates a vicious cycle that feeds the chaos.

- Smoothly nesting random-length, random-start projects is like putting together the pieces of different jigsaw puzzles. Even if you somehow get a fit, as soon as one project gets behind, chaos returns.

- People can't get used to a rhythm, so experience doesn't tell them what to do. They don't know how quickly to converge on solutions, how much detail they should have at each point of the process, or who needs what kind of information at a given time. So, they have to be told what to do. But the people telling them what to do don't know either, so they generate more chaos.

- Because the situation is constantly changing, it is impossible to improve anything. What we learn one day is useless the next.

- Over-loaded people skimp on some kinds of learning, so projects run into trouble and are over schedule. People learn to rely on others being late, and therefore are late themselves.

So how can you solve these problems? How can you provide people with a stable environment so that they can learn from experience and exercise initiative? How can you level demand on resources?

It's easy to establish a cadence. Start projects at standard intervals, and finish them at standard project lengths.

More precisely:

1) *Classify your projects by type*, identifying the kind of question each project type will answer.

2) Determine a *demand time for each type*—how often you need a project of that type for each product line.

3) Determine an *allowable lead time for each type*—the time available between starting the project and finishing it in order to satisfy customers.

4) Set a *cycle time*—usually the shorter of the demand time and the allowable lead time.

5) Set a *cadence time*, usually the same as the cycle time. Move toward starting and finishing a project each cadence, using SBCE and adjusting objectives and resources as required in order to make the deadline.

6) *Nest the projects* together to level the load on resources.

7) Push this cyclic, cadenced process down into the projects themselves, for each resource. Stable, rhythmic, cyclic processes within each project are really the big win—but you can't get them unless the project schedule is stable, rhythmic, and cyclic. *Project launch is the pacing process* that sets the cadence for the whole development organization.

FYI: Definitions

Demand time: how often you must run a project in this product line in order to keep up with customer needs and technical progress.

Allowable lead time: how long you can afford between an opportunity arising in the market or the technology and starting to manufacture.

Cycle time: how long it takes to actually conduct a project.

Cadence time: the actual interval between starting new projects.

Let's do an example. Suppose you are an automotive parts supplier, making, say, oxygen sensors. You classify your projects into research, tailoring or applications focused on projects, and strategic breakthroughs. (See the discussion under "Set-based concurrent engineering" on Page 111.)

Development Project Classification

You get six or so **application** projects each year. Each project may involve a new connector; some specialization of the electrical ground arrangements; and a minor change in coatings on the electrode. Each project answers the question, *"What is the best way, within the constraints of our current manufacturing system and product family, to satisfy this particular customer?"*

The demand time is two months. The allowable lead time is a little more vague. The customer usually wants prototypes and a frozen design within one year after settling on the specifications, with full-rate production a year later. So (Step 4), you should set the cycle time at two months. You should start a project every two months and finish two months later.

"Wait," you protest. *"Why should I try to finish my projects in two months, when my customer would allow me to take two years?"* Here's why.

- Your customers will love it, because it removes a major uncertainty and provides the knowledge they need much earlier; or, if you start later, you will have the most up-to-date information available.

- You get a chance to improve your process and your product, with a complete learning loop every two months instead of every two years.

- You know that you have the resources to do a project every two months because you are doing a project every two months on average. But you are wasting people now, either by staffing multiple projects in parallel, or requiring people to jump back and forth mentally from project to project, and you won't have to man many projects in parallel.

Now the big one. "*Wait,*" you say. "*I just can't do it that fast. There are long lead times here.*" Well, maybe. If you look closely, I bet you will find that half the lead time is consumed administratively conducting the change process, going through a purchasing procedure, waiting in a queue to get prototypes built, waiting for tests, etc. The other half comes from not sticking closely enough to the definition of a tailoring project, trying something too innovative, and having it bite you, or having to design, build, and debug new manufacturing equipment. So if you set two-month cycles as your goal, you'll be forced to get rid of a lot of this waste.

The only likely reason you can't shorten the cycle is that the knowledge isn't available fast enough; specifically, your customers can't tell you what they want fast enough. You may be able to address this problem by getting ahead of them, figuring out what they need before they tell you. Or you may find that once you have a stable cycle going, you can quickly learn to cut your cycle time to a month, and go through two iterations with each customer.

Or, at worst, perhaps you do have to drag the process out. If so, try to set aside a period each week—say, Tuesday afternoon—when everyone involved works on this process. Tell the customer and suppliers you are doing this, and call them every Tuesday afternoon. Review the documents. Do what needs to be done. And set the project aside for another week.

Now let's look at **strategic breakthrough projects**. Breakthrough projects answer the question, "*What is the best manufacturing system and family of products to support my family of customers and beat my competition for the foreseeable future?*"

To understand the demand time here, you have to ask, "*How often is there something really new in this product line? Something that requires new manufacturing processes or new knowledge about the product? Something that the other products can't compete with?*" For automotive products, the answer might be, "on average, every four years." To answer the question, go back and look at the history. How often have significant innovations come along? The future likely will be similar.

For strategic breakthrough projects, the lead time usually is shorter than the demand time. You probably need to be able to incorporate opportunities that arise up to, say, two years before start of production. So, your project cycle time should be two years.

Now you have a hard choice. Breakthrough projects require much larger teams than **applications** projects because they generate a lot of new knowledge, considering many ideas in parallel in order to guarantee success. You can set the cadence at two years, keep a team steadily busy, and devastate the competition by doubling the frequency of breakthroughs. Or, you can save money by using a four-year cadence, and rotating the team between two different (preferably related) product lines. The team still will be busy doing a project every two years—just for different products.

In either case, remember to rotate people off and on the team when the team switches projects, not in the middle. You'll need to move people back and forth between breakthrough and tailoring projects. Try not to just disband the team after each project though. They've learned how to work together, and you don't want to lose that. It's O.K. to have a person working on more than one team—but efficiency starts to decline as soon as they are working on more than two. (You may have to spread some scarce resources very thin—we'll see later how to do it best.)

Adjust your objectives and the size and skills of the team to get done on time while still making an adequate breakthrough. You have to learn enough at each breakthrough to move a little faster than the rest of the industry, knowing that you will make breakthroughs at the cadence rate. If really exciting ideas come up, you may have to pull people from elsewhere in the organization.

What if there is an emergency—you just finished your breakthrough project, and the competition comes out with something that blows your new products away? Spend a few minutes kicking yourself for having missed the opportunity—obviously, your set of alternatives wasn't big enough. Then, treat the emergency as an emergency. Cancel the project you had planned next for the team, and do another project for this project line.

Research projects need the discipline of cyclic cadence even more than other kinds of projects, because it is so easy for researchers to wander aimlessly forever while producing nothing useful. To set a demand time, think about how many new concepts you will need to feed into your strategic projects in order to be confident of success. Crudely, if you usually have four subsystems plus the system in your products, you are doing a strategic project every four years for each product line; you have four product lines, and you need 10 ideas for each subsystem; you need 50 ideas a year, one per week. So, demand a new, evaluated idea each week from your research department. (If they are insulted by your efforts to make them "create to schedule," point out that all successful creative artists work to a similar discipline.)

Once you have stable cycle times and a cadence for projects, you have predictable, similarly shaped building blocks for your overall plan. You can start nesting them together to level resource loads (Step 6). For example, Toyota nests vehicle development, engine development, and manufacturing system development roughly as shown below.

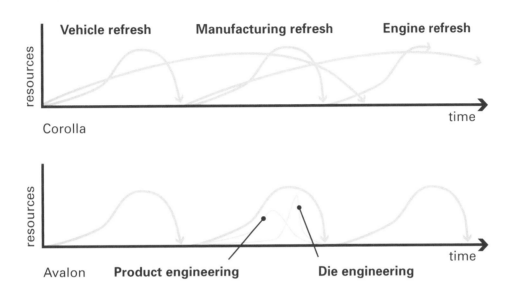

Because manufacturing system and engine developments have about half the demand time of vehicle development, there are two vehicle development cycles for each engine or manufacturing development cycle. Engine and manufacturing projects are staggered to level the integration demands on the chief engineer—each car program usually deals with only one or the other. And the chief engineer can handle two different product lines because only one project is using significant resources at a time.

(Engine development, at least, also has a minimum cycle time about twice that of vehicle development. This is not a coincidence. Cycle time tends to drop to meet demand time, because people work at it. And technology-driven demand time tends to rise to equal cycle time, because your competitors often can't go any faster than you can.)

Finally, looking at the bottom of the figure, we get a preview of our later discussion of resources cycles, and we see why Toyota has each engineer work on multiple projects. Engineers must have beginning-to-end responsibility to avoid hand-off, but major demands on their time may last for only a few months, as in the case of die engineering.

Die engineers have more projects each than product engineers, because most projects at any given moment involve the die engineer only in design reviews and periodic meetings. The resource cycle problem is to get these different demands on a cadence, reducing interruptions and load variations to a minimum.

Before we address that, however, we need to push the cadence down inside the development projects—the subject of the next section.

Quick cycles: Pull and flow of small knowledge batches

How can we organize engineering activities so that people know what to do next, and aren't being constantly yanked around by circumstances and the demands of others? How can we get knowledge to the right place at the right time?

Lean companies create a web of small, constantly operating, rapid, cadenced cycles.

Why cycles? Cycles create *dynamic order*. Complex moving systems always involve cycles, from the four-stroke cycle of an engine to the heartbeat of the body. Without cycles, every situation is brand new, and there is no order.

Cycles are natural in factories because the basic mass production processes all are short cycles: stamping, repetitive assembly, etc. Even so, lean manufacturing works hard to maintain the cadence. Cycles are much harder to maintain in development because they are longer, and every cycle deals with new knowledge and actions.

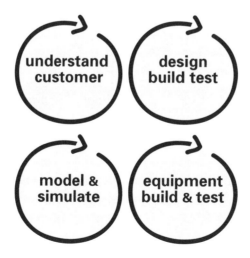

"Aha," you say, *"Everything in development is always new. My developers are creative artists. You can't expect to run development to a standardized routine."*

Actually, it won't run well any other way. Take two cases that are more extreme than development:

- Combat is the most chaotic, highly variable environment faced by humans. An intelligent enemy is actively trying to destroy your order, down to the complex cyclic cellular and tissue cycles that constitute life. Successful militaries counter by routinizing, standardizing, and putting to a cadence everything they possibly can, so they can focus on handling the unavoidable variation. That is why soldiers wear uniforms.

- Painting, composing music, and writing literature are, at their best, even more creative than development. But every successful artist I know about had an extremely standard routine for creating, starting at the same time every day, using the same tools, usually in the same room. The rest of their lives may be chaotic, but their work is as disciplined and consistent as a bricklayer's. When I am writing, I find I go fastest if I work in 45-minute-to-one-hour cycles, interrupted by 15 minutes of administration or exercise.

Development cycles are not completely stable. They are subject to variation caused by new knowledge. They are constantly being improved. The emphasis of activities changes during projects, from more emphasis on understanding the customer at the beginning to more on constructing and testing production equipment at the end. We aren't trying to eliminate variation caused by new knowledge. A design process that does exactly the same thing every time is useless. But we are trying to eliminate variation that we cause for no good reason.

We want:

- People to know when they will see each other.

- To work on every aspect of the design every week.

- People to "automatically" know what to do because they have been in their current situation before.

- People to have time to do what they should be doing.

The cycles are small and fast so that they will produce knowledge in small batches. The knowledge is abstracted into trade-off curve sheets and exchanged at regularly scheduled meetings, allowing "customers" for the knowledge to "pull" it from an "information field" as needed. (One Toyota manager said, "The secret of our success is that anyone at Toyota can talk to any one else as needed to get information.") We'll discuss how to maintain good information fields when we get to the "team of experts" concepts later. For now, note that information fields are visual and easily accessed by anyone.

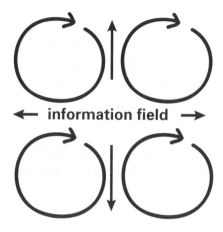

Conventional thinking tries to produce large batches of knowledge according to a schedule and move those batches through channels. For example, conventional thinkers imagine they can prevent problems by completely formulating specifications at the beginning of a project because developers will "have all the needed knowledge" before they start designing. Similarly, conventional batch manufacturing may try to produce a month's supply of a part in one set-up. Lean thinking recognizes the costs of such large-batch processes. Large-batch production in the factory creates inventory that must be transported, stored, and managed; allows defects to go unnoticed until they have been replicated many times; and requires production to a schedule, resulting in over- and under-production with concomitant expediting and rush orders. These more than negate the advantages of infrequent changeover.

Specification   **Product system design**   **Detailed design**   **Test**   **Equipment design**

The situation is much worse in development. For example, doing all the specification at the beginning of the project creates several problems:

- The batch process creates uneven demand on resources, which is difficult to manage efficiently. Specification demands a lot of time from customers and the organization members who best know the customers. Trying to cram this time into a short period creates massive disruption, preventing the smooth flow of operations. Attempts to plan for this disruption always fail because the schedules never stabilize.

- The batch is hard to handle. The specifications must be read and understood; developers get bored and miss vital details. In the same way, the large batch of parts shipped by a conventional supplier must be stored somewhere until it can all be used.

- The batch process allows defects to accumulate. Problems with the specifications often are unnoticed until someone tries to design based on them, just as factory defects often are unnoticed until the part is used.

- The "inventory" of knowledge represented by the batch depreciates rapidly. Technologies and customer needs change. By the time the project is finished, it may be obsolete.

- Because conventional developers or operators do each activity infrequently, they forget how to do it; the required tools have wondered off or gone out of adjustment; the required habits of interaction are lost. This causes quality problems after batch production changeovers. It's worst in development, which has longer cycles. The people with experience may have moved.

- Finally, most development interactions need to be two-way. We cannot finish specifying a product without a partial design because the design itself determines some of the aspects to be specified. For example, we may attempt to write a purely functional specification for short-range vertical takeoff military transport aircraft. If the contractor attempts to achieve the specification using a twin-engine tilt rotor design, we will need to add a new requirement addressing the ability to operate in formation, because such craft are highly vulnerable to turbulence from their neighbors.

Development needs continuous flow of small batches even more than factories!

SBCE operates through cycles, linked by the narrowing process, knowledge bases of trade-off curves, and weekly (or sometimes daily) meetings. The entire process is replicated for the subsystems. The cycles operate concurrently for every level of the system, for product and manufacturing engineering, for supplier and OEM. Thus, the complex sequential systems of mass development are replaced by a simple structure of concurrent, similar building blocks. Big blocks—system designs—are made from smaller blocks—subsystem designs. But every block essentially is the same, and they all can go on continuously.

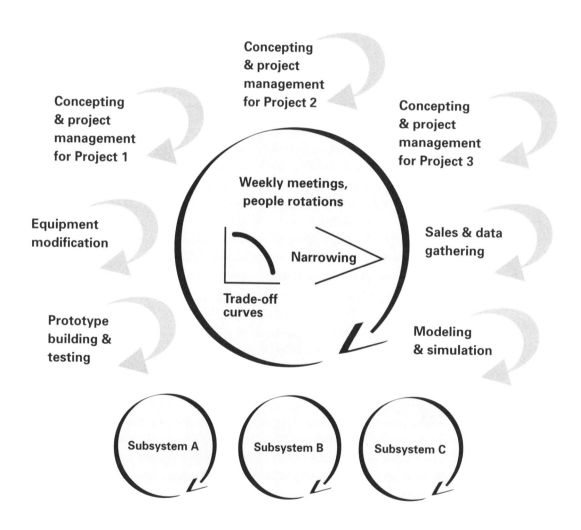

These cycles are not synchronized. The prototype building and testing, modeling and simulation, sales and data gathering, and subsystem development cycles are partially independent from concepting. Simulation may investigate a number of variations on a concept, building trade-off curve knowledge to support a number of different projects. Subsystem designers may produce subsystem concepts that can be used to support a variety of system projects.

This frees every part of the organization from the need to wait for other parts. Test engineering can be testing at the same time product engineering is designing; and manufacturing engineering can be developing new concepts. Suppliers and subsystem designers can be developing their concepts simultaneously with system designers. And Sales and Marketing can be using partial prototypes and test data to check for customer reactions.

This asynchronous method makes sense for large, breakthrough projects involving a significant amount of innovation, and where innovation at the subsystem level can be relatively independent of system-level innovation. On the other hand, suppose you are conducting a series of application projects but don't have the manufacturing-limit curves well defined. In this case, you might build the whole system around getting one afternoon every two weeks in the plant in which to build prototypes on actual production equipment. This ensures that you are designing and selling a product that you actually can make in quantity. All the cycles would be tightly synchronized to the prototype build cycle.

Honda uses such relatively tightly coupled cycles for engine development. A Honda engine program typically involves eight complete cycles through prototyping; one per quarter. The early cycles address the most critical requirements on the engine and its parts; later cycles deal with less-critical issues.

To define cycles, pay attention to what you are actually already doing. Identify:

- *a question* to be answered

- *cycle and cadence times* (usually the same, and you may need to find demand and lead times first)

- *a responsible owner* who will work to keep it on track

- *ways of exchanging information* with its customers/suppliers (usually the same people); this may involve trade-off curves, weekly meetings, drawings, prototypes, etc.

- *a time-line map* to show how and when the cycle resources will interact

- *a resource list of people* who will participate, with the approximate fraction of their time they expect to devote to the cycle

As soon as you identify cycles, improve them. One fuel-injection project team leader was able to shrink the time required to design, make, and test a part from about four months down to one day! Use timeline maps to identify waste in the cycle, and eliminate it.

Pay particular attention to the waste of waiting. For example, prototypes waiting to be tested represent tied-up knowledge, which depreciates rapidly. The knowledge that is invaluable now frequently is nearly useless in a month because we have already made the mistake it might have prevented. So, we need to reduce the time between knowing what we want to build and test and actually building and testing it as much as possible. Prototype labs need substantial excess capacity, and there should be no administrative delays between deciding on the design to be tested and getting the test results.

You will see your entire organization becoming more efficient as the chaos drains from the process. People will be able to spend their time adding value rather than fighting crises, planning, or chasing each other down.

Be careful not to overload people. To start with, people should reserve at least 50% of their time free of any cycle to handle the activities that aren't yet under cyclic control.

 ### Implement cycles within projects

Start with pilot projects. Hold workshops to identify the cycles, decide on a coupled or decoupled strategy, and plan the implementation. Use waste-elimination techniques to reduce your cycle times. At first, you may shorten the cycle times at every pass through the cycle.

We've been learning to establish a cadence from the top down, establishing a project cadence, then supporting cycles. Now we've arrived at the level of the individual resource and are ready to learn how to dramatically improve communications and the fraction of time devoted to useful work. In the process, we will put to an end the controversy over "project team" versus "departmental" organization.

Individual resource cycles

Every company faces the same problem. Putting people physically next to each other dramatically improves communications. Co-located development teams may go twice as fast as their physically distributed counterparts.

But everyone needs to communicate with at least two groups: their project team and their fellow specialists. Otherwise, departmental learning stops, and the wheel must be re-invented for every project. Parts, suppliers, and manufacturing processes proliferate. Co-location usually leads fairly quickly to the loss of expertise and common cross-team approaches. Chrysler saw major gains in the late 1980s, but began having considerable difficulty with its development process by the late 1990s. And many people have to support many different project teams; duplicating them would simply be too expensive.

So how do you balance the need for close communication within teams and within specialties? How do you ensure that a person who supports many different teams provides effective support to each? How do you reduce the effort team members expand tracking down such support people? How do you achieve the advantages of co-located, dedicated teams, together with the advantages of a strong departmental structure?

Simple. You put everyone on a rotating cycle that supports every assigned project once a week.

For example, have purchasing agents spend, say, one hour each Tuesday and Thursday with each team they support in the team war room. Standardize and publish the hours. There is then no need for engineers to harass purchasing at other times. They know their needs will be met within two days.

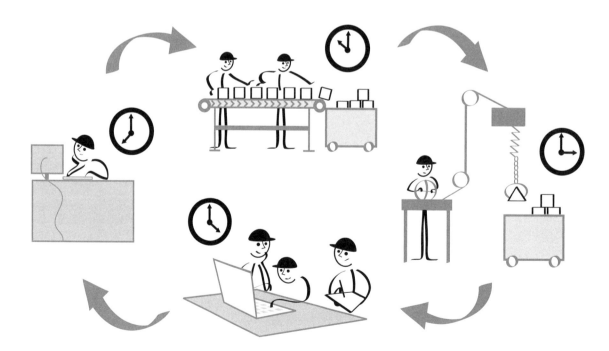

Hitting every project every week (or day) at a scheduled time is much easier psychologically than trying to finish one project first because you don't have to worry about what may be falling through the cracks—you know you are doing the most important aspects of every project frequently enough. The consultants at Toyota Supplier Support Center reserve Fridays for office work, visiting clients no more than four days a week.

Support this by minimizing the importance of location. Issue laptops instead of desktop computers, cell phones instead of desk phones. Consider wireless Internet access. Make all information accessible electronically, everywhere. Provide a war room for each team, where sample parts are available. Team members should spend regularly scheduled periods of time together in the war room, working on their individual responsibilities but available for quick crosschecks of information.

Rotate resources on larger scales as well. For example, Toyota assigns some plant personnel to project teams about one year before product launch. They retain their plant loyalties, and rotate back to the plant with the product. The chief engineer on products being designed partly in the United States rotates back and forth between countries as frequently as every two weeks.

To make rotations work, bosses have to exercise restraint about reassigning priorities. There are real emergencies that require disrupting the schedule—but in general, these need to be minimized. However, building in frequent "administrative" periods can help deal with short-term demands, smoothing the flow.

Such rotations retain the cross-project learning advantages of departmental organization, but gain the advantages of team organization:

- Priorities at any given moment are clear: "Right now I'm working for team X. Tomorrow, I'll be working for you, and I'll take care of your problem."

- Formal and informal communication—information spreading by "eavesdropping"—is easy because people spend appropriate amounts of time in physical proximity. No one has to be chased down in order to exchange knowledge.

- There is little waste of waiting or scatter from expediting, because people adjust to each other's schedules, and work on appropriate parts of the project to provide needed knowledge at the assigned time.

Implement individual cycles

This actually is very easy, but it is unfamiliar, so you'll have to teach people how to do this. Make sure that management understands the basic concept and promises to support it. Hold workshops with development teams and departments to try to negotiate appropriate amounts and times of support. Publish the schedules. Monitor. It is easy to backslide.

Information pull

How can people get the knowledge that they need, when they need it, without being bombarded by knowledge they don't need? How can people function effectively while moving from place to place? How can you get rid of the waste associated with information channels?

You need good information fields, arrangements of information that make it as easy as possible for people to pull the information they need. Good information fields make everything that isn't creative as simple and easy as possible, so that people can spend their time creating. More precisely, as much as possible, people should be able to find the information and material they need at a glance, a few keystrokes, or at worst a short walk.

Expert craftsmen build their own tools, organize their own shops, and invent their own methods—after learning from their predecessors in the craft. Toyota carries this principle into the factory, where operators follow "standardized work sheets" with a precision Frederick Taylor (the father of scientific management) only dreamed about—but design the standardized work themselves. Lean developers are responsible for organizing their own work, and everyone in development needs to practice two basic skills:

1. Organizing the physical environment to make information obvious.

2. Organizing the electronic environment to make information available and reliable.

To organize the physical environment, first get rid of everything you don't need, including dirt, junk, old equipment, unneeded space and inventory. Discard, clean, or repair. Set aside a chunk of time each week for the purpose. Five-S books on factory lean can help.

This is important because all this stuff represents *bad information* that distracts and misleads the development team. Dirty, cluttered, or damaged surfaces attract the eye, which spends a fraction of a second trying to pull useful information from them every time we glance past. Old equipment hides the new equipment from the eye and forces people to ask which to use.

Organize what is left. Put together the things that are used together. Keep the manuals with the equipment (appropriately protected). Keep the screwdrivers with the screws, and the trade-off curves and reference books with the design engineers. Don't be afraid to duplicate the commonly used tools and references; the few dollars you save by having only one copy of everything quickly will be devoured by the time it takes expensive engineers to visit the library.

But organize everything. The effort required to organize will encourage people to get rid of the materials they don't need. Label everything and the place it goes, and put it in place. Why rely on memory to tell you whether things have been put away? Why force people to look in many places to find something?

Establish a cabinet with office supplies within easy reach of every office, so that people don't need to hoard office supplies themselves. At the front of the shelves put magnetic strips labeled with the supply type, cabinet name or number, and the number that should be on hand. Post instructions: "When the supply quantity falls below the number on the magnetic strip, drop the strip in the envelope on the door." Assign someone to pick up the strips and buy new supplies daily.

To check out tools and equipment, provide each developer with magnetic strips with their names on them that they can leave in place of the equipment.

Organize workspaces in cells to shorten the distance between people and the information they need. Establish a standard layout for workspaces, so that someone temporarily assigned to a team can easily find materials and information. Keep things compact. Excess space gets filled with clutter that hides useful information.

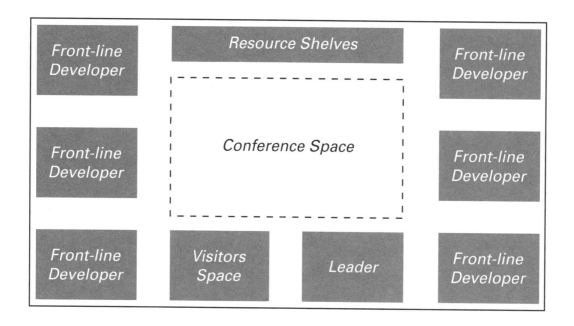

Development involves a lot of "short run" activities; for example, producing a batch of prototypes. Where possible, make things mobile so that you can easily reorganize to have the right materials readily at hand. Put workbenches and desks on wheels, so you can reorganize readily to work on different projects. Put machines on wheels or provide overhead cranes or forklift access so they can easily be moved around. Provide local or plug-in dust-and-chip collection.

All this requires effort, but it pays off in reduced effort in the long run. You are trying to put as much knowledge as possible "into the environment" so that it is immediately accessible, without undue effort or the need to rely on memory. Physical organization is easy to see and can get people excited about lean.

Put key information in the physical environment where it is available at a glance. Use large format printers to make it easy to maintain the same information on the wall and electronically so that it can be accessed from anywhere, but people are reminded of it in appropriate places.

FYI: Simple ways to make information visible

- Post in the halls a status board showing the target events, or at least the launch date, for each project, with the project leader's e-mail address. Let the project leader color code the projects green, yellow, or red. Provide the reason for red or yellow codes and the corrective action being taken.

- At the entrance to every work area, put a chart showing where people sit, their pictures, what they are working on, and where they are physically located now. Color code the parts of the building, and post building maps and/or sign arrows at all major intersections so that people can easily find resources. Assign someone to keep these up to date.

- Post the capabilities of test equipment in the hall outside the lab.

- Post examples of current and future design processes.

- Mount an old lap top computer on the wall of each meeting room, programmed to act as a "meeting cost clock." The meeting leader enters the number of people supposed to be in the meeting and the start time. The computer multiplies the time since start and the number of people by the standard personal cost rate (generally around $50 to $150 dollars per hour) and displays the resulting costs.

- Maintain project team "war rooms," with sample and competitive parts, and posters of critical information. This may include issue lists, comparison matrices of alternatives under consideration (and competitor's solutions), cost, weight, performance and timing targets, as well as the cost of delay, weight overrun, and performance shortfall.

- The appropriate organization of electronically provided knowledge is a vast subject, and an opportunity to institute information pull far beyond Toyota's current capacity. Here are some concepts:

    Establish a single electronic document and a single owner for every piece of information. You can have different people owning different parts of the document, with one person taking overall responsibility. You can have multiple windows into the same knowledge base, with different people looking at different pictures. But, you need to be clear about who is responsible for each kind of knowledge, and you need to have only one place for that knowledge.

The goal here is:

- *Anyone can get any required information from any physical location at any time.*

- *There is only one copy of every piece of information, and one owner, so we don't have conflicting versions floating around confusing people.*

The problem is that our basic concepts of management were formulated in the typewriter age. Typewriters and carbon paper could make a few copies of information, which had to be pushed through carefully designed channels to make sure the right people got the information. But that meant that people were responsible only for the information they received; if they didn't get it, it was someone else's fault. This created magnificent opportunities for delay, finger-pointing, bureaucratic empire building, and confusion.

There is no longer any reason to have channels; all the information in the company can be universally available, unless security concerns prohibit. People can be held responsible for checking periodically the information they need, or they can be automatically notified of changes.

- Keep documents short, preferably one page or a computer screen. Provide electronic links to back-up and connected documents.

- Make changes easy to find, and provide either automatic notification, a repetitive checking method, or a notification list. Automatic notification may require some programming. Repetitive checking is easy if documents are kept on a shared drive. People can simply sort the documents by modification date and check the ones that have changed. To maintain a notification list, just let people add their e-mail addresses to the list, indicating that they want to be notified if the document changes. The person making the change copies the list into an e-mail address.

- In any case, show changes in a standard way, perhaps with lines in the margin. Remove the lines on a standard day each week or month, so that people know how often they have to check.

- Make the priorities for software ease of use and reliability. Get people what they really need to do the job. Be careful about buying massive, special purpose, do-everything software; it rarely works well, and it tends to force people to do things the way the software designer envisioned. You want your software to support your process and people, not dictate solutions to them. The people who will use the product, not the information department, must have first say in what you buy.

- Get rid of manual re-entry. Nothing should ever be typed twice. If your systems are so incompatible that you can't do automated translation, change them.

- Support engineers with engineering tools. Engineers need to sketch, form three-dimensional geometry, and do mathematical derivations. Conventional office software is inadequate for these purposes.

- Don't get too attached to legacy systems. Yes, you have all that data on the current system. But how much of it is actually used? You probably spend more each year maintaining the legacy system than a simple off-the-shelf replacement would cost. Legacies tie you to doing things the wrong way.

Implement information fields

You will need to run a lot of workshops to re-organize local areas and teach people what to do. Create opportunities to show off what people have accomplished—this both teaches and encourages.

Assign every kind of information to an owner. Let the owner figure out how to make the information available.

Hold periodic "town-hall" meetings to argue about software and knowledge organization. Everyone is vitally interested in this topic, and everyone needs a voice.

It is finally time to turn to the foundation of the whole system—the skills of the individual developers and the way you build those skills.

Implement the whole system of cadence, pull, and flow

Start anywhere that is easy. Keep up your momentum by continuing to broaden and deepen your efforts. Involve the whole organization.

Teams of responsible experts

To understand the "team of experts" concept, imagine that you need open-heart surgery. You investigate two different surgical hospitals.

At the first hospital, you meet a surgeon. She says, "*I will be completely responsible for your case. I have done 4,321 of these operations, and expect to do thousands more. I've always wanted to be a surgeon, and keeping you alive and enhancing the quality of your life is the center of my professional existence. I conduct my own research on surgery, publishing a paper every few years, as well as read everything available in the literature. My success rate is three times the average. My team has done at least two surgeries together per week for the past three years. All members are experts in their own right, except for one apprentice surgeon whom I will closely supervise. As you can easily see by watching them, they are completely focused on working together to achieve the best possible result for you. Your case is somewhat unusual. Let me explain the complications that may occur, and how we will deal with them.*"

At the other hospital, you meet an administrator. The administrator says, "*All of our surgeons have graduated from top medical schools. To make sure we get the best, we have promised them that if they do a good job, they can move quickly out of surgery and into administration. To broaden their experience, we move them around rapidly; in fact, during your surgery, you can expect to have at least two different lead surgeons switch off. This works because our procedures are the most detailed in the world—the surgeons just need to follow the procedures for everything to go perfectly. Whenever a patient dies, we improve the process to make sure it won't happen again. In fact, we assign an administrator to each surgical team to make sure the surgeons are doing the right things, and to coordinate between the surgeons, anesthesiologist, and nurses. The administrator is responsible for making sure that your surgery meets our high standards. Thus, we can assemble our surgical teams at random, and the different specialists can focus on their own areas of expertise without worrying about needing to communicate with each other. We keep detailed metrics on the performance of every specialty. For example, our surgical nurses are required to reduce material use by 5% every year. We reward them with bonuses if they do. I'm sure that your surgery will go exactly according to our process; you have nothing to worry about.*"

Who will you let cut open your chest—the team of responsible experts, or the bureaucracy?

Is it possible for an organization to change from a bureaucracy to a team of responsible experts? Yes. I've watched the U.S. Army do it, during six years of active duty and seven in the reserves, and as a member of several National Academy of Sciences panels advising the Army.

The Army I joined in 1973 had been shattered by Vietnam. Drug use and racial friction were rampant. Officers went into some barracks only when armed and in pairs. The Army's fundamental ethos had failed. The Army had been the ultimate "can-do" bureaucracy: obedient, structured, and hierarchical, with a procedure and a plan for everything. That approach had not delivered victory in Vietnam, despite overwhelming technological advantages. Fifty-eight-thousand dead had been sacrificed to little apparent benefit.

That Army rebuilt itself into a "team of experts" that won the Gulf War (the first Gulf War, 1991) with only a handful of casualties. In my mind, the Army's success completely refutes claims that there is something uniquely Japanese about Toyota's success. The basic principles are the same.

Both Toyota and the Army avoid the waste of hand-off, carefully uniting knowledge, responsibility, action, and feedback. Both have built an extraordinary level of discipline based on responsibility and self- and mutual respect. Both largely have replaced bureaucratic management with strong, expert, mission-focused, and value-creating leadership.

Let's begin with the basic behavior we want our people to exhibit; then ask what leadership approaches, skills, organizational structures, and personal policies are required to produce these behaviors.

The behaviors: responsibility, teamwork, expertise

In a lean organization, how do you want people to act? You want them to take responsibility, to work effectively in teams, and to develop real expertise.

Responsibility must be for contribution to the success of the project as a whole—for results, not just for their own specialties or for doing what they are told. Automotive stylists, for example, must be artistically creative, with a good sense of what will excite customers. But they also must be concerned about the impact of their work on manufacturing cost and quality. And manufacturing engineers must constantly seek to expand their capability to support more interesting product designs.

Teamwork requires explaining knowledge to teammates, listening carefully to the teammates' thoughts, and negotiating toward solutions that are good for the system as a whole. Good team players honor their contracts, doing what they say they will do.

They both speak out whenever their expertise and judgment are needed, and loyally support the team's decision once made. They must be able to support and participate in many teams at once—their departmental team, several development teams, and perhaps an ad hoc team or two aimed at a specific problem. Teamwork also requires a common language, a shared way of talking and thinking about problems, so that people can understand each other.

Expertise is developed by continual learning and decays rapidly when learning stops. This requires reading appropriate technical material and observing and asking questions about the work of others. But real experts also learn directly from experience; their new knowledge is embodied in frequently revised trade-off curve sheets.

So how do you get there? We've actually talked about most of the things you need to do, but there are a few more concepts to learn.

Responsible Experts

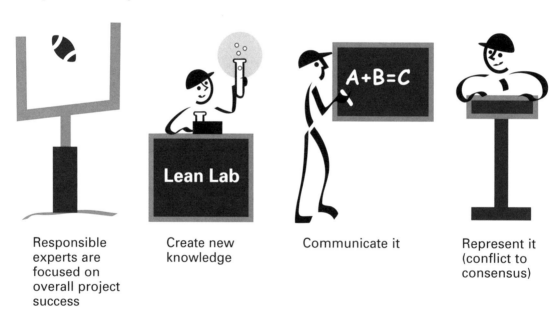

Responsible experts are focused on overall project success

Create new knowledge

Communicate it

Represent it (conflict to consensus)

Leadership for effective discipline

Have you ever said that your organization has an undisciplined development process? Are your people divided between those who argue that all of the problems arise because of a lack of discipline and those who claim that development is a creative art and discipline kills it? Both viewpoints seem correct. How can you reconcile them?

By noting that there are two definitions of discipline, and two ways to achieve it. External discipline means that they'll do whatever they are told. Tyrannies such as the old Soviet Union enforce external discipline by reward and punishment, including summary execution. External discipline produces rigid, clumsy organizations and angry, unhappy people.

Internal discipline means that people do the right thing as they see it. Internal discipline is the foundation of some recent remarkable successes of the U.S. Army—and of Toyota. It produces efficient, flexible organizations, and proud, happy, productive people.

Creating internal discipline demands much more from leaders than external discipline, which is why it is so rare. In particular, you first of all will need to avoid the waste of feedback, by giving your people:

- *clear, distinct, and complete areas of responsibility*. (Otherwise, they are subject to so much second-guessing that they stop doing the right thing and wait for orders —or there are so many conflicting decisions from over-lapping responsibilities that nothing gets done.) We've talked about making someone responsible for each document and piece of information. More importantly, make someone responsible for each part. Never tell anyone what to do; instead, require them to explain what they believe they should do, and why.

- *the opportunity to actually take direct action* to accomplish those responsibilities through their own work. (Otherwise, they just are telling others what to do, and we are back to following orders. Conventional management unites responsibility and authority; lean management unites responsibility and action.) This means that engineers should design their own parts, do their own analysis, and create their own trade-off curve sheets to the greatest extent possible, not rely on CAD operators and an analysis section to do it for them.

- *the knowledge required to decide to make the decisions and execute the actions*. This includes deep technical expertise and an understanding of how the parts fit into the whole.

- *objective, direct-from-reality feedback* on how well their decisions work out. (If the feedback is on how well their bosses like the decisions, we are back to compliance and external discipline.) The Army provides this feedback most clearly through the National Training Center in California, where large units fight realistic battles using lasers to simulate weapons. The "enemy" wins most of these battles—and every engagement is analyzed in excruciating detail to see what can be learned.

Similarly, development teams must remain with their projects through launch, and must carefully analyze success and failure. All developers, but especially project leaders, must be evaluated first of all on the success of the projects in which they have participated.

FYI: Lean product development leadership behavior

- *Leaders must focus on generating success for the organization rather than on allocations of blame.* Back to the National Training Center for a moment: I'm told that the first three brigades to rotate through were badly beaten by the opposing force, which used Soviet tactics and was assigned permanently to the Center, gaining an overwhelming experience advantage. The Army (the story goes) relieved the brigade commanders of command. After ruining the careers of three of its very best, however, the Army realized that every brigade was going to lose, and began focusing instead on learning as much as possible from the defeats.

- *Leaders must provide clear, consistent, and workable visions* of where the organization is trying to go. (The Army calls this "the commander's intent," and has redesigned its procedures for writing operations orders to minimize detail and emphasize the commander's intent.) This allows people to make decisions on their own, knowing that they will support the overall mission.

- *Leaders must demand and exemplify ethical behavior above all.* Telling the truth, honoring agreements, providing honest service to customers, and of course obeying the law are not merely good PR. They are the foundations of effective performance because they provide a constant framework within which people can make decisions knowing that they are doing the right thing. They enable people to live in a morally rational universe, in which effect follows cause. Conversely, rewarding salespeople who successfully lie to customers soon leads to an impossibly confusing situation, in which lies are "good" sometimes and "bad" other times, depending only on whether the customer happens to catch on this time. (The Army not only evaluates leader's ethics but has embedded ethics training at every level of its extensive school system.)

- *Leaders must be visible, easy to communicate with, and worthy of respect.* Good military leaders command from up front, and good development leaders spend the majority of their time in laboratories, test facilities, and design offices. They look over shoulders, ask questions, and listen and respond honestly to requests for support.

- *Leaders must respect and care about their people.* This implies demanding high standards but enforcing them thoughtfully and respectfully. (On its way to excellence, the Army eliminated the time-honored use of physical punishment.) It implies telling the truth and paying careful attention to the truth when people speak it (even if their understanding of the truth differs from yours). Always assume first that people are doing their best, and only ignorance or a failure in the system caused the bad result; only repeated failure should lead you to question an individual's desire to excel.

- *Leaders must set the example.* People pay far more attention to what their leaders do than to what they say. If leaders are curious about product failures, developers will learn from them; if leaders punish mistakes, people will hide them. If leaders spend their time fighting fires and ignore the long term, so will everyone else. If leaders duck the hard problems, so will others. If leaders shoot the messenger, bad news will be hidden.

- *Leaders must be authentic.* Tactfully say what you really think, intend, and feel. Organizations that function by pretense and fear have a very hard time learning, because reality is constantly being obscured—and keeping it obscured takes tremendous effort.

- *Above all, leaders must be useful.* People follow leaders who can help them efficiently accomplish what they are trying to do, and they bitterly resent leaders who distract them with irrelevant or petty demands. Departmental leaders create expertise through trade-off sheets and teaching. They help out as needed. Project leaders design the system. Both are creative, contributing to the formation of the new knowledge the team needs to succeed.

 DO

Implement effective leadership for internal discipline

Start a leadership school. Effective leadership behavior does not come naturally to most people. Both the Army and Toyota have an extensive system of internal schools in which they teach people how to perform effectively in the job they are moving into. Use role playing among peers to teach the principles we've discussed. They aren't complicated or hard; they are just different.

Efficient, effective communications

Knowledge is not enough. Xerox, AT&T, General Electric, and GM created the finest research laboratories in the world—and derived very little benefit from them. So how can you make knowledge usable?

Teach your people to communicate effectively and efficiently.

Efficiency is critical. Studies show that managers in some conventional companies average 2.5 hours daily dealing with e-mail and voice mail; most of this time probably is waste. Other studies show that engineers may spend more than half of their time looking for information. And most people in conventional companies report that meetings consume a very large part of the working day.

Conversely, when Jeff Liker and I did a survey of automotive suppliers, two results stood out. First, Toyota's suppliers had a very high opinion of Toyota. Only 5% reported significant problems working with Toyota, versus 25% of suppliers to other Japanese companies, and 50% of suppliers to U.S. auto companies. Second, Toyota's suppliers met less often with their Toyota counterparts than the suppliers of any other company.

There are four keys to better communications:

1. Use semi-standard, usually one-page formats.

2. Focus on essential facts and logic.

3. Use the appropriate medium—words, numbers, drawings, graphs, and equations.

4. Prepare for and conduct meetings efficiently.

Let's look at each in turn.

1. Use semi-standard one-page formats

Conventional organizations are apt to use a large number of long forms. Lean organizations boil these down to very few one-page formats. This makes them easy to understand and use. If the user needs to modify the form, they do so.

Boiling things down to a single page helps the writer really think through the issue. A U.S. supplier to Toyota provided 80 pages of data on a quality problem. The Toyota engineer sent it back with a note: "Reduce to one page. Then you will understand the problem." Communicate the big picture; provide references to details.

We've seen the most important one-page format, the trade-off curve sheet. Another very important format, the problem-solving sheet, follows the standard problem-solving approach:

1) Review the background.

2) State the problem.

3) Analyze the cause.

4) Present the alternative solutions.

5) Recommend the best solution.

6) State an implementation plan.

7) State a feedback plan, to assess how well the solution works.

This format often is called an A3 report. Adapt these formats to a wide variety of circumstances, rather than creating new formats.

2. Focus on essential facts and logic.

Many companies operate largely in never-never land. They devote great effort to plans, procedure statements, budgets, business cases, programs, slogans, visions, and internal advertising. All these deal with how things should be, or how we want them to be. All are needed, but they should be kept brief and simple, and we should not spend much time on them because they are not real. Spend the time on the reality, understanding what is actually happening, analyzing what is actually possible.

3. Use the appropriate medium—words, numbers, pictures, graphs, equations.

Use visual information—pictures, graphs, and visually structured documents—as much as possible. The brain processes visual information much better than any other kind. When Mike Masaki, president of Toyota USA, was asked for the secret of Toyota's success, he said there were two: the one-page problem-solving format, and the fact that all Toyota engineers draw.

Most U.S. engineers don't draw. Provide classes and tools, but above all, cure people of the notion that drawing badly is an excuse for not drawing at all. Just do it, and do it, and do it; ignore deficiencies in appearance, focus on the knowledge being communicated, and insist on pictures in almost any circumstance.

Operating Computer-Aided Design systems is an important case. Conventional companies often have CAD departments, but most lean design engineers shape geometry directly. Their CAD models are slower to build, and less pretty and uniform than those made by CAD specialist—but they can get the whole development done much faster. The American who headed interior design for the first Camry designed jointly between Toyota's Technical Centers in Japan and the U.S. believed that eliminating CAD operators halved development time. English is a poor tool for defining geometry. The communication between design engineer and CAD operator is slow. (Of course, many CAD operators are skilled enough to take on the entire design function; stop worrying about who has what degree, and let them do the work.) Treat ease-of-use and availability to all developers as primary in selecting CAD systems.

Equations are nearly as important, and the cure is the same: just insist on seeing the math. Perhaps because of the influence of business schools, U.S. companies blunder about trying to solve an incredible array of problems using words, when simple mathematical analysis would make the situation infinitely clearer.

4. Prepare for and conduct meetings efficiently.

Meetings are a very poor tool for communicating information. They don't provide a usable permanent record, people usually haven't thought the issues through very well by the time of the meeting, and anyone who isn't there misses the information.

Provide information through durable, one-page, living, electronic documents. Use meetings to resolve confusion and conflict. Before the meeting, require everyone to have already looked at the relevant documents, and have the meeting only if there is a need to resolve issues.

When meetings are necessary, there are some keys to making them effective and efficient:

> *Always surface conflict.* We asked one Toyota Chief Engineer, "What makes a great car?" "Lot's of conflict," he answered. Conflict often occurs when everyone is honestly representing their points of view. Absence of conflict usually means that someone is not speaking up, and therefore some vital knowledge is being omitted. The trick is to create an environment in which conflict is expected but is handled calmly and with curiosity instead of defensiveness. The curiosity leads to shared knowledge, which leads to creativity and agreement.

Conduct win-win negotiations. Everyone in lean development is responsible for representing their unique expertise, making sure that the product and manufacturing system are as good as possible based on the knowledge they have. But everyone is responsible for system success, not just the success of their components or success from their perspectives. Thus, everyone should be committed to achieving "win-win" solutions that look successful from every perspective.

Focus on fact and logic. I can't over-emphasize this. Once we begin trying to make decisions on the basis of power, once we stop listening, once we start repeating our arguments instead of paying attention to the other person's, we've lost. It doesn't matter what the authorized procedure is; it doesn't matter if we've already invested a lot; it doesn't matter what the boss says. Only the facts and logic matter.

Treat everyone's thoughts and feelings, including your own, with respect. Pay attention to what you, and other people, actually think and believe. If someone says something that doesn't make sense to you, say, "That doesn't make sense to me." Then, listen very closely to their explanation. Offer your own thoughts. But don't assume that you are right. In fact, assume that you probably are wrong—that the other person, within the zone of their own expertise, is more likely to be right than you are.

Go see, ask why. Looking at actual problems, exploring actual alternative solutions, analyzing actual causes, often produces the possibility of a win-win solution where none appeared before.

Teach people to communicate effectively

This takes classes, for everyone, and they may have to be repeated yearly. It's best if you can go down the chain of command. After the classes, the chain of command must continue developing everyone's skills.

Establish a culture of authenticity, in which people routinely say, *"I really don't understand. Can you put it on one page, in a picture or equation?"*

Personnel management for expertise and responsibility

How can you manage promotion, training, and assignments to enhance the team of responsible experts?

Toyota offers a marvelous example.

First, all Toyota developers (and other white-collar employees) spend about half of their first year assembling and selling cars. This insures that every developer has a basic understanding of both the final customer and the factory—the customers for the development process. It helps keep developers focused on adding real value as perceived by the customer.

Most U.S. companies think they cannot afford such a long preparation. So, they have every white-collar employee spend one day per quarter in the plant, directly adding value. Such experience can help break down the social barriers between the most important members of a company—the operators in the plant—and those who should support them. (Such social leveling is standard in the U.S. Marines—every Marine, even pilots and accountants, is an infantryman first.)

Second, Toyota identifies the critical skills associated with each job. First-line supervisors track the employee's demonstration of these skills at four levels:

- *Understands the basic principles.* Engineering knowledge is the foundation of success. Engineers who are not good at engineering are moved to other jobs rather than allowed to hide behind other skills.

- *Works fast enough to keep up with the team.* This requires understanding how to efficiently apply the basic principles to achieve a good solution quickly.

- *Takes responsibility for the work.* Until developers have achieved the third level of skill, they normally will be required to explain every significant action to their supervisors. Once they have achieved the skill level required to take responsibility, they can decide for themselves whether they need to check their actions with others.

- *Can teach the skill.*

Level three—readiness to take responsibility for the work—allows the extraordinary speed and flexibility of Toyota's decisions and processes. Responsible developers can decide, for example, whose signatures they need on an engineering change. The result:

A client of mine built a transfer line for Toyota. While planning the line, he saw the opportunity for major savings if a small change could be made in the part. He called the manufacturing engineer in Japan, who said, "I need to talk to the product engineer. I'll get back to you in one hour." One hour later, the manufacturing engineer called to say, "The change is approved."

Engineering changes in large conventional companies normally take at least several weeks, because the change form must past through an extensive arrangement of channels, accumulating signatures as it goes. The difference is that the Toyota engineers were responsible for knowing who they needed to talk to before making the change. In this case, they or their supervisors were able to determine quickly that the change would not affect anyone else.

Thus, responsibility—and the decision-making freedom that goes with it—becomes a reward for study and hard work. Toyota empowers its employees perhaps more than any company in the world—after they have demonstrated the specific ability to handle that power.

Ability to teach the skill is the key to leadership success. Usually, a first-line supervisor should have demonstrated the ability to teach most skills in the section. This is easier than you may suppose because Toyota, like the U.S. Army, avoids most of the overhead of conventional teaching lectures, showmanship, and test preparation.

The U.S. Army also clearly identifies the skills associated with each job, and evaluates, hands-on, each individual's (and unit's) ability to accomplish those skills. Such "performance-oriented training" helps convert from external- to self-discipline, placing the responsibility for expertise on the individual. In contrast, conventional training programs—which require a certain number of hours per year, for example, or reward people who obtain advanced degrees—emphasize the role of the teacher. The employee may learn nothing useful at all.

Instead, the Army teaches by a simple process.

- The teacher demonstrates the skill.
- The learner performs the skill, and the teacher critiques the performance, until the learner has mastered it.

Medical interns learn by a similar "watch one, do one, teach one" process.

At Toyota, the demands on the learner are even greater. Often there is no explicit demonstration, and the critique is by questioning the learner until the learner discovers for himself where his error is.

For example, when a newly hired engineer is assigned to a functional department (after working in a plant and a dealership), he is assigned a mentor. Mentors usually are skilled engineers with eight or so years of experience; success as a mentor is important in proving one's potential for management. The mentor finds a problem for the new engineer to solve outside the department, so that any difficulty the new engineer has will not affect his career. (22 Assignments are sometimes within the new engineer's department.)

Even if the new hire is a product engineer, the problem normally involves some large greasy machine that is not working properly. The mentor introduces the problem; shows the new engineer to a desk and telephone; points out the reference library; and says, *"Don't do anything without talking to me first."*

Because new engineers are accustomed to homework assignments, they usually soon arrive at a solution to the problem. After they outline it to the mentor, the mentor says, *"Who have you talked to about the problem?"* The answer of course is, *"No one."* The mentor is likely to simply nod and wait. Eventually, the light dawns: *"Of course, I should talk to the operator. I'll go now."*

"Wait," says the mentor. *"What will you ask the operator?"*

Most new engineers try to make up questions on the spot. The mentor suggests, *"Why don't you go back your desk and think through your questions completely."* When the engineer returns, the mentor asks detailed questions: *"Why will you ask that? What physical principle underlies this question? What are the different possible root causes of the problem? How will your questions enable you to determine which is the actual cause?"* When the mentor is satisfied, the engineer will be allowed to go ask the questions.

Most new engineers return excited, with a new solution to a problem. The mentor listens, then asks, *"Who else should you talk to?"* Smart engineers quickly understand: *"I need to talk to the maintenance mechanic. I'll go make a list of questions."*

Questioning later turns to the details of engineering theory, with new engineers justifying their beliefs in great detail, complete with references. Whenever the new engineer suggests a root cause or a solution, the mentor asks, *"What other possibilities exist? Why do you think this is the right one?"*

By the time the questioning is finished, new engineers have a very clear understanding of how to think through a problem the Toyota way: gathering data, posing alternative explanations in solutions, and conducting tests to determine which alternative is best. (Of course, this is the scientific method.) The mentor then permits the new engineer to execute the engineer's preferred solution, even if the mentor prefers a different solution. Engineers must trust their own judgment and understand that Mother Nature, not any human being except customers, is the final judge of their work—so they must be allowed to make mistakes.

Once the problem has been solved, the mentor turns the new engineer over to the departmental team leader, who says, *"Here is the problem you will be working on. Don't do anything without talking to me first ..."*

This Socratic process of teaching by questioning can be infuriating. Socrates knew the key to success: sincere curiosity. The questioner must be genuinely interested in the answers, listen to them carefully, think about them, and respond openly. *"I don't want to tell you what to do, but I'm uncomfortable with your picking a solution without considering more alternatives. Have you considered alternatives X, Y, and Z? What are their advantages and disadvantages?"* is very different from *"That's not the right answer. Guess again."*

The third major element of lean personnel management is keeping people in position long enough to become expert and to get good feedback on their decisions. This can be a fairly short period of time. The Wright brothers taught themselves to build a flying machine in only five years. But it must normally include several complete design cycles, and it must preclude any possibility of getting by without real expertise through good social skills. (The Wrights designed and flew a complete machine at least every year, made numerous redesigns, and conducted extensive series of experiments on parts of the system.)

Toyota career paths are somewhat different for area specialists and system designers—but senior executives can come up through either route. System designers—engineers with the potential to be project leaders—normally will receive a broader range of assignments, grooming them to represent customers and converse fluently with a wide range of specialized developers.

Fourth, lean companies require engineers to "get their hands dirty." Engineers need to build some prototypes and conduct some tests themselves. One learns much more quickly that way. Toyota believes so strongly in this principle that it has a "silly vehicles contest" in which engineering departments design and build vehicles to a single guideline—they must be useless. This allows engineers to get their hands dirty without slowing down regular development programs.

The hard choice is between "engineer playground" shops and allowing engineers into the main prototype shops. The latter often is preferable if the personality of the person running the shop supports it. Educating engineers and making them clean up after themselves while conserving their expensive time and maintaining peace between them and the "real" technicians is a tricky balancing act. Many shop managers can't handle it. Engineers also need to play their part: Respect, courtesy, good work habits, and the occasional case of beer help.

Finally, and most importantly, developers must be evaluated on their contributions to project success. The most important parts of a personnel record are a list of demonstrated skills and a list of projects worked on, with their profitability. In addition, managers must be alert to developers' reputations among their peers. Thus, assignments should be determined by a cross-functional board of senior developers, able to ask their subordinates, "What did this person contribute to these projects?"

The alternative is to let managers simply hire the people they want. With a good cycle of support running, managers can be expected to pay attention to reputation and record on contribution to projects.

 Implement lean personnel management

Start by tracking project success; this is easy. Getting people into the plants merely requires courage. Identifying required skills takes time and effort; have the departments work on it, frequently comparing notes.

Time now for the hard stuff—the underlying psychology of lean development.

"A system for grownups"

John Shook, the first American employed by Toyota in Japan and a profound lean thinker, originated that wonderful phrase, "It's a system for grownups." Jim Womack put it this way, "Lean is hard because it is a system for making mistakes instantly visible, and most people hate that."

But Toyota people don't hate it; they love it, and can't imagine working any other way. What is the psychological shift?

Succinctly, "grownups" learn to value "power-to" over "power-over."

To understand the difference, we can place a good lean project leader at the power-to end of the spectrum. Good project leaders are fanatical about creating a better product. Often, they have no other ambition. They influence the entire organization by their expertise, their enthusiasm, their skill at listening, and their ability to solve problems. They constantly seek the power-to convert their dreams into reality. They take joy in creating value.

At the other end, we can place Joseph Stalin or Adolph Hitler, men who pursued power-over other people for its own sake and were willing to sacrifice all other values to achieve it.

Somewhere between lies the stereotypical empire-building bureaucratic manager. Empire builders continually seek to have more people placed under their control. They teach nothing, in order to maintain the power that comes from unique knowledge. They seek power-to make decisions, but usually decide "no," so that they cannot be held responsible. They start projects and advocate wonderful new techniques and organizations—but arrange to be transferred before results of the changes can be seen. Or, they homestead in a position from which they cannot be displaced. They strive to maximize the metrics by which they are evaluated (and the size of their bonuses), playing games with numbers regardless of the effect on creating value. They refuse cooperation to other departments, enjoying their ability to make others jump through hoops to obtain support. They abuse suppliers and toady to customers, often taking contracts that cannot be profitably fulfilled.

Note that both kinds of person seek power. Power-seeking is a basic human trait, essential to survival and developed by evolution—powerlessness in the natural world is quickly followed by death. Lean organizations do not try to create self-sacrificing, power-avoiding saints. Instead, they emphasize the advantages to the individual of seeking power-to instead of power-over—and to the organization of rewarding high performance with power-to rather than power-over.

First, power-to means power to create value. Organizations that help people achieve power-to naturally create more value. Because human beings enjoy creating value, each employee also benefits. And, of course, the organization survives and profits, which is usually good for the employees! Working in a conventional organization means, sooner or later, dealing with the threat of extinction.

Second, everyone can have power-to, whereas only a few can have power-over—by decreasing the power—the freedom—of the rest. Organizations that reward people by increasing their power-over soon find that most people become discouraged and unhappy. They also find themselves trying to fake people out by creating absurdly top-heavy organizations, trying to create the illusion of power-over (I worked once in a 100-person company that had 15 vice presidents.)

Third, power-over is emotionally and organizationally self-defeating. The more we depend on our power-over others, the more we depend on them—and the more helpless we feel. This is one reason Stalin and Hitler became increasingly paranoid as their power increased, seeing plots against themselves everywhere. Sometimes they were right, because power-over naturally creates resentment. The resentment leads to the "powerful" leader not being able to achieve his goals, which creates the desire for more power-over, which creates more resentment, which leads to trying harder to impose power-over by force, which ... mass murder is the logical consequence of the fearfulness that leads to the desire for power-over. In most companies, the resentment does not lead to planting bombs—but it does lead to slow work, avoidance of responsibility, elaborate blame-assignment drills, poor quality, rapid personnel turnover, etc.

Our desire for power-over is rooted in childhood. Parents have (and need) power-over children, and children perceive them as more powerful than they are. Children do not see their parents work—exerting power-to—and therefore form a distorted picture in which all value flows from power-over rather than power-to. They learn that happiness is given by the powerful. And they learn that they can get their own needs met by exerting power-over their parents, manipulating them through an impressive variety of strategies, beginning with crying.

In fact, children are hard-wired to manipulate their parents. They respond to parental attention long before they are even aware of the physical world. This is, again, evolution. Historically, many people died in childhood, and any edge in getting parental support was very strongly selected for. So, the lessons of childhood are astoundingly persistent. We act them out long after they no longer make sense. Adults commonly seek power-over and the favor of the powerful even though this behavior makes them unhappy.

They put their energy into:

- developing spectacular presentations

- responding instantly to requests from superiors (even when they don't create value)

- trying to guess at the their superior's motivations

- trying to associate themselves with people who look like they will succeed

- advocating the winning position in any conflict

- avoiding conflicts they might "lose"

- avoiding data that might make them "lose"

This is an exhausting, miserable way to live. Even the most powerful people who take this approach to life commonly see themselves as victims. And they are; but they don't realize that they are victims of themselves. (It's O.K., though. They compensate by making miserable anyone they have power over.)

Much conventional management theory (and even more practice) relies on this behavior to achieve "control"—more accurately, the illusion of control. Companies prescribe processes, punish process violations, establish metrics, hold status reviews, send exhortations over voice mail or e-mail, establish change programs, isolate "high-potential, fast-track" favorites, and use evaluation forms mostly based on social skills such as "communicates well" (read "gives great presentations") and "reliability" ("does what I tell her").

You will need to make a real effort to break down this immature behavior and replace it with mature behavior—behavior oriented on creating value rather than on compliance or appearances. We've seen the tools already:

- *Track the actual results achieved.* What projects has this person supported? How well did those projects do?

- *Look at the actual work done.* Many organizations distinguish between design reviews, in which experts look at the actual work, and gate reviews, in which managers review the developer's promises. (*"Are you going to meet the cost target? Have you completed the assigned tasks?"*) How absurd that the people who have the power to reward look only at the illusion of performance.

- *Gather a broad but informal range of opinions about performance.* Formal all-around rating schemes simply provide another opportunity to game the system, but informal questioning of co-workers—particularly co-workers in other departments the individual has supported—can be much more useful. Again, the question needs to be, *"What has this person done or not done to support you?"* not *"Is this a nice guy?"*

- *Ruthlessly suppress all consideration of where or whether someone went to school* once a person has been hired. If degrees are useful, the results will show up in performance—any other consideration should be simply a matter of personal pride.

- *Invert the organization chart, so that managers and executives support the people who actually create value*—plant operators and line developers. Cultivate a general organizational respect for knowledge—power to—and the creation of value. Uphold the creators of value as the organization's heroes, listen to them daily, and treat them with consistent respect.

- *Relentlessly push for a fusion of technical skill and business savvy.* Development managers who do not retain or develop technical expertise should be sent to manage something else. Technical experts who don't care about money or people should be assigned to front-end research and required to develop new knowledge to a regular cadence, or assigned to trouble-shooting teams.

- *Appropriately monetarily reward value creation.* The difference in productivity of a good engineer compared with a mediocre one probably is a factor of 10; the difference in pay is more likely to be 10%. The most straightforward way to provide monetary rewards for creating value is to provide a bonus to the entire team based on the profitability of each project. No profits—no bonus. Alternatively, as in Japan, bonuses can be given to everyone based on the performance of the entire company. But bonuses should not be based on any metric that can be gamed—because it will be.

So let's finish with the most fundamental question of all: *What's in it for you?*

Did I surprise you? Were you expecting some idealistic exhortation about why to do lean development?

No. The only good reason for you to invest your effort in lean development is that it is good for you. How will it be good for you?

I *hope* it will make you more successful in your company if you aren't already the CEO. But I can't guarantee that. You may run into powerful people who hate and fear these ideas, and therefore will hate and fear you. And I *hope* it will make your company more successful. But unless you are the CEO, those same people may block any useful change. You can influence these effects (we'll discuss how in Part 4), but you can't control them.

But there is one benefit that you can control completely. Lean development is a careful elaboration of a single idea—***learn from reality***. And learning from reality has the great advantage of enabling you to live in a rational universe.

Conventional approaches always wind up frustrating people. Even if you can get them adopted, they won't work because they are based on a distorted picture of reality. They require you to believe impossible things, such as that you are smart enough to tell your subordinates exactly what to do. They create unpleasant, endless, useless conflict as part of the endless struggle for "power-over."

Lean approaches, on the other hand, are based entirely on observation and logic. Their objective is "power-to"—and enhancing my power-to usually enhances yours, rather than reduces it. So they enable you to approach any situation calmly and happily, knowing that whatever happens, you will learn something, and you will be able to try to do things that make sense.

Try it. I'm quite sure you'll like it.

Part 4: Starting the Change

Congratulations! You know how to measure success and identify wastes, and you have an overview of the complete system. But how will you make such a large change in your organization?

You won't. *Change will occur when the majority of people in the organization have learned how to see things in a new way.*

That is, change is a learning process—just like development! In fact, the same principles you have learned for developing better *operational* value streams can also be used to develop better *development* value streams.

Focus on creating value as perceived by the customers of the change—the developers. Change always has to be supported from the top, but if it has to be imposed on developers who believe it is counter-productive, something is wrong.

Provide leadership that cuts across departmental boundaries—and get agreement from departmental leaders to support the change. Pull the organization forward with the tension between the current situation and what you are trying to achieve.

Explore multiple solutions, keeping and spreading the ones that work.

Maintain momentum with a cadenced, repetitive cycle of change with pull from target events.

Draw on the entire team of experts. Get representatives from all the parties interested in development involved, and listen to them carefully; seek consensus and data. Look for results—a better value stream—not compliance.

How does this translate into action? Here are the things you need to do. You will probably have to do them more or less simultaneously, little by little, as in any learning operation, because they interact.

1) *Get widespread, general agreement on the problems* with the current situation, especially at the top of the organization.

- Examine your organization's performance on the metrics of Part 1. Your goal is to establish a reason to change. If you adopted the lean system, how much better could your company be? Spread this knowledge as far as you can, as fast as you can, with hall posters, newsletters, Web sites, briefings, or anything else that will work.

- Analyze your current system for waste as in Part 2. If you have a box-and-arrow description of your process, use it as a starting point. If not, draw a time line chart. Again, publicize this.

2) *Build through discussion a general vision of where you want to go.* You need a critical mass of the company to at least partly understand and be excited about the lean development concepts.

- Use Part 3 as a basis. Buy everyone a copy of this book, or hold workshops, or both.

- Expect and encourage controversy, disagreement, and argument. Take it seriously and use it to move toward understanding. Form users groups or discussion sections, or talk about the concepts during staff meetings or over lunch, or discuss objectives for change up and down the organization—but have a discussion, don't just issue orders.

- You don't need perfect agreement, or perfect understanding—but you need enough understanding to tell whether any given move is in the right direction. This is more important and harder than it sounds. People who have spent their lives learning to see things the conventional way naturally will twist the lean concepts around to fit the way they already think—and wind up doing exactly the wrong things.

3) *Find people who want to lead change.* They can be part time or full time, informally or formally designated, but they need to want to stick with it long enough to develop and spread real expertise. They need to be effective communicators, and they need to grasp the basic concepts intuitively. Usually, they are people already pretty frustrated with the current system (people who like the current system don't want to change it). But, they need to be comfortable with changing by teaching rather than by commanding.

4) *Pick things to change and get started.* Pick something you think some part of the organization is ready to do—hold a waste-elimination workshop, start using trade-off curve sheets, start a lean project. Pull together the people who need to do and support this work. Have them read the relevant sections of this book. (Give them the whole book; they'll need the rest later.) Brainstorm and plan how to implement the concept, and do it.

5) *Establish a cadence.* Try to do something at least every two weeks: hold a waste-elimination/process redesign workshop, start a new team going along lean lines, hold a meeting to compare notes on how things are going, conduct a review with the executive staff, have a workshop with an outside speaker, review the trade-off curve sheets in a department ... something. Just go through this book and pick out things from the "to do" tasks you think your company is ready to implement somewhere, and start implementing them. You need to "constantly spread the virus, or the organization's immune system will kill it, and things will go back to 'normal'," in Jim Luckman's wonderful analogy. Have each project also work to a cadence, reviewing its own progress every month or so.

6) *Launch an expanding torrent of lean projects.* Don't try to convert projects that are already started. It is too hard to change directions. But treat every new project as a potential opportunity. Whether to actually go ahead with lean depends partly on whether the organization can absorb the rate of change, but mostly on the project leader's personality. Good candidate project leaders find the lean ideas intuitively exciting and are mentally flexible and eager for responsibility.

7) *Let the project leaders design their own processes* (but *strongly* encourage them to learn from each other and move toward a common process). Provide "release from standard process" letters to cover them while experimenting. Later, write simplified processes capturing what the project leaders actually did.

8) *Surface and resolve conflicts between project leaders and departmental or functional managers in special meetings.* Let the project leaders talk about what they need and support them. The only reasons for a department head not to do what a project leader wants are it's unsafe; it won't work; it will make it harder to support another project leader. And the department head owes the project leader an explanation and a compromise solution.

9) *Create opportunities to share knowledge.* Have project leaders talk about what they are doing to run their projects better, design better systems, and take responsibility for profit. Have department heads talk about what they are doing to build the knowledge base and support projects. Have individual developers talk about what they are doing to organize their work and workplaces.

10) *Don't be afraid to ask for help, but be careful who you ask.* There are a lot of ignorant consultants in the world; check the source of their knowledge and the quality of their reasoning. There are no real experts in lean development; even Toyota developers, who understand it at a gut level, can't necessarily explain it very well. But whoever you pick should challenge your intuitions, be open about what they know and don't know, and help you think things through.

So there it is; the complete system; you've made it through the book! Hope you found the concepts as exciting as I did, and can't wait to go create better development systems.

Acknowledgements

I will never know every person that contributed to my father's work. However, I will try to acknowledge those I can and for those I miss, please know that my father thanks you even though I cannot. I am deeply grateful to John Shook, friend, colleague, and editor who resurrected the work from scattered CDs and tirelessly prepared the book for publication. Durward Sobek, a long time student, colleague, and friend of my father's, continually contributed to his work not only in this publication, but in the ideas that compelled my father to write the book. Constantly challenging him and providing an exciting forum to debate ideas were my father's students and colleagues. Walid Habib, Jeff Stein, the late John Long, Tom Shuker, Jim Luckman, Beau Keyte, and Eric Vasser were just a few of the many colleagues that shaped my father's life. I'd also like to thank Steve Rubin, a friend and confidant whose advice and guidance gave my father the confidence to pursue authorship. And most of all, in speaking for my father, I'd like to thank his wife and life-long friend Yasuko, who convinced my father to leave the Army to go to MIT, take a professorship at the University of Michigan, and then leave academics to pursue his dreams. Without her, none of this would have been possible.

Henry S. Ward